S0-FBD-286

Teaching
Black Cinema

Peter Jones

Series Editor: Vivienne Clark
Commissioning Editor: Wendy Earle

British Library Cataloguing-in-Publication Data
A catalogue record for this guide is available from the British Library

ISBN 1 84457 1564

First published in 2006 by the British Film Institute
21 Stephen Street, London W1T 1LN

Student worksheets to support this guide are supplied at: www.bfi.org.uk/tfms
User name: **blackcine@bfi.org.uk** Password: **te2007bl**

Design: Amanda Hawkes
Cover photograph: Denzel Washington in *Malcolm X*, courtesy of *bfi* Stills
Printed in Great Britain by: Cromwell Press Ltd

www.bfi.org.uk
The British Film Institute's purpose is to champion moving image culture
in all its richness and diversity across the UK, for the benefit of as wide
an audience as possible, and to create and encourage debate.

Contents

Introduction to the series

Since the introduction of the revised post-16 qualifications (AS and A2 Level) in the UK in September 2000, the number of students taking A Level Film and Media Studies has increased significantly. For example, the latest entry statistics show the following trend:

Subject & Level	June 2001	June 2002	June 2005
A Level Film Studies+	2,017	–	–
AS Level Film Studies	3,852	–	9,188
A2 Level Film Studies	–	2,175	4,913
A Level Media Studies*+	16,293	–	–
AS Level Media Studies*	22,872	–	32,346
A2 Level Media Studies*	–	18,150	23,427

*Three combined awarding bodies' results
+Legacy syllabus – last entry June 2001
(Source: *bfi* Education website – AS/A2 statistics refer to cashed-in entries only)

Changes to the 14–19 curriculum are currently in development for 2008 and will doubtless see further increases in the number and take up of courses in this subject area.

Inevitably such increases in student numbers have led to a pressing demand for more teachers. But, given the comparatively recent appearance of both subjects at degree level (and limited availability of specialist post-graduate teaching courses), both new and experienced teachers from other disciplines are faced with teaching these subjects for the first time, without a degree-level background to help them with subject content and conceptual understanding. In addition, the post-2000 specifications saw the arrival of new set topics and areas of study, some of which change frequently, so there is a continued need for up-to-date resources to help teacher preparation.

I meet a large number of Film and Media Studies teachers every year in the course of my various roles and developed the concept and format of this series with the above factors, and busy and enthusiastic teachers, in mind. Each title provides an accessible reference resource, with essential topic content, as well as clear guidance on good classroom practice to improve the quality of teaching and students' learning. We are confident that, as well as supporting the teacher new to these subjects, the series provides the experienced specialist with new critical perspectives and teaching approaches as well as useful content.

The three sample schemes of work included in Section 1 are intended as practical models to help get teachers started. They are not prescriptive, as any effective scheme of work has to be developed with the specific requirements of an assessment context, and ability of the teaching group, in mind. Likewise, the worksheets provided in the online materials offer examples of good practice, which can be adapted to your specific needs and contexts. In some cases, the additional resources include online, such as interviews and illustrative material, available as webnotes. See www.bfi.org.uk/tfms.

The series is clear evidence of the range, depth and breadth of teacher expertise and specialist knowledge required at A Level in these subjects. Also, it is an affirmation of why this subject area is such an important, rich and compelling one for increasing numbers of 16- to 19-year old students. Many of the more theoretical titles in the series include reference to practical exercises involving media production skills. It is important that it is understood here that the current A Levels in Film and Media Studies are not designed as vocational, or pre-vocational, qualifications. In these contexts, the place of practical media production is to offer students active, creative and engaging ways in which to explore theory and reflect on their own practice.

It has been very gratifying to see that many titles in this series have found an international audience, in the USA, Canada and Australia, among others, and we hope that future titles continue to be of interest in international moving image education. Every author in the series is an experienced teacher of Film and/or Media Studies at this level and many have examining/moderating experience. It has been a pleasure to work so closely with such a diverse range of committed professionals and I should like to thank them for their individual contributions to this expanding series.

Vivienne Clark
Series Editor
May 2006

● Key features

● Assessment contexts for the major UK post-16 Film and Media Studies specifications
● Suggested schemes of work
● Historical contexts (where appropriate)
● Key facts, statistics and terms
● Detailed reference to the key concepts of Film and Media Studies
● Detailed case studies
● Glossaries
● Bibliographies
● Student worksheets, activities and resources (available online) – ready for you to print and photocopy for the classroom.

● Other titles available in the series include:

● *Teaching Scriptwriting, Screenplays and Storyboards for Film and TV Production* (Mark Readman);
● *Teaching TV Sitcom* (James Baker);
● *Teaching Digital Video Production* (Pete Fraser and Barney Oram);
● *Teaching TV News* (Eileen Lewis);
● *Teaching Women and Film* (Sarah Gilligan);
● *Teaching World Cinema* (Kate Gamm);
● *Teaching TV Soaps* (Lou Alexander and Alison Cousens);
● *Teaching Contemporary British Broadcasting* (Rachel Viney);
● *Teaching Contemporary British Cinema* (Sarah Casey Benyahia);
● *Teaching Music Video* (Pete Fraser);
● *Teaching Auteur Study* (David Wharton and Jeremy Grant);
● *Teaching Analysis of Film Language* (David Wharton and Jeremy Grant);
● *Teaching Men and Film* (Matthew Hall);
● *Teaching Film Censorship and Controversy* (Mark Readman);
● *Teaching Stars and Performance* (Jill Poppy).

● Forthcoming titles include:

● *Teaching TV Drama*; *Teaching Short Films*; *Teaching Film & TV Documentary*.

SERIES EDITOR: Vivienne Clark is an Advanced Skills Teacher of Film and Media Studies at Langley Park School for Boys, Beckenham, Kent. She is currently an Associate Tutor of *bfi* Education and Principal Examiner for A Level Media Studies for one of the English awarding bodies. She is a freelance teacher trainer, media education consultant and writer/editor, with several published textbooks and resources, including *GCSE Media Studies* (Longman 2002), *Key Concepts and Skills for Media Studies* (Hodder Arnold 2002) and

The Complete A–Z Film and Media Studies Handbook (Hodder & Stoughton 2007). She is also a course tutor for the *bfi*/Institute of Education MA module, An Introduction to Media Education Practice.

About the author:

Peter Jones teaches A level Film and Media Studies at Queen Mary's College, Basingstoke, and is an examiner for WJEC Film Studies. Before becoming a teacher he worked in the film and television industries, and as a journalist.

Introduction

Assessment contexts

	Awarding body & level	Subject	Unit code	Module/Topic
✓	AQA A2 Level	Media Studies	Med 4	Texts and Contexts
✓	AQA A2 Level	Media Studies	Med 5	Independent Study
✓	AQA A2 Level	Media Studies	Med 6	Comparative Critical Analysis
✓	OCR A2 Level	Media Studies	2734	Critical Research Study
✓	OCR A2 Level	Media Studies	2735	Media Issues and Debates
✓	SQA Advanced Higher	Media Studies	DV32 13	Media Investigation
✓	WJEC A2 Level	Media Studies	ME4	Investigating Media Texts
✓	WJEC A2 Level	Media Studies	ME5	Changing Media Industries
✓	WJEC A2 Level	Media Studies	ME6	Text and Context
✓	WJEC AS Level	Film Studies	FS3	Messages and Values
✓	WJEC A2 Level	Film Studies	FS4	Small-scale Research Project and Practical Application of Learning
✓	WJEC A2 Level	Film Studies	FS6	Critical Studies
✓	CCEA A2 Level	Moving Image Arts	A2 1	Creative Production and Research Advanced Portfolio
✓	Edexcel BTEC National Diploma	Media (Moving Image)	Unit 37	Film Studies

This guide is also relevant to the teaching of film in Lifelong Learning and international courses. The following titles in this series would be useful companions to this one:

- *Teaching World Cinema*. Detailed background on non-Hollywood cinema from around the world, focusing on France, Scandinavia and Hong Kong.

- *Teaching Analysis of Film Language and Production*. A full exploration of film language and how to analyse films, as well as production methods.
- *Teaching Contemporary British Cinema*. Particularly relevant to the AQA, OCR and WJEC A Level Media Studies specifications, and especially WJEC's A Level Film Studies specification, as well as to Scottish Highers and Advanced Highers.

● Specification links

Teaching Black Cinema will help teachers following a specification with a Hollywood and/or UK cinema approach, as well as aspects of World cinema.

AQA Media Studies A2 – Med 4: Texts and Contexts
Representation, genre and the film audience are the key concepts for which this book can provide examples in black cinema.

AQA Media Studies A2 – Med 5: Independent Study
Political, social, economic, historical and institutional influences or audience issues relating to black film are all possible areas of study relevant to this coursework paper.

AQA Media Studies A2 – Med 6: Comparative Critical Analysis
Cross-cultural comparisons, mainstream and alternative variants (eg of topics, representations, audiences, ideologies etc) are a major focus of this synoptic paper.

OCR Media Studies A2 – 2734: Critical Research Study
Women and Film is an optional topic for which black cinema study may provide useful material.

OCR Media Studies A2 – 2735: Media Issues and Debates
All three section B topics may be addressed by a study of this book: Contemporary British Cinema, Genre in Film and Censorship and Film.

SQA Advanced Higher Media Studies: DV32 13 – Media Investigation
This book could provide relevant examples for the independent research and analysis required.

WJEC Media Studies A2 – ME4: Investigating Media Texts
There is wide scope in this coursework paper for almost any form of media research and analysis, but particularly comparative study of two texts, eg *Shaft* (1971) and *Shaft* (2000).

WJEC Media Studies A2 – ME5: Changing Media Industries

Several topics and case studies contained in this book could offer material for the Film and Cinema option.

WJEC Media Studies A2 – ME6: Text and Context

The specified genre from 2007 is crime, for which the study of blaxploitation and black new wave films would be helpful, as well as such British films as *Bullet Boy* (2004) and *Rollin' with the Nines* (2006).

WJEC Film Studies AS – FS3: Messages and Values: British and Irish Cinema

Burning an Illusion (1981) and *Bullet Boy* are both close study options for 2007–8.

WJEC Film Studies A2 – FS4: Small-Scale Research Project and Practical Application of Learning

This guide offers numerous possibilities for projects on stars/performers, genre (eg blaxploitation), and social, historical and/or political context (eg slavery, Black Power). Spike Lee, Charles Burnett and Keenen Ivory Wayans are possible candidates for auteur study. Many aspects of black cinema are possibilities for the film journalism option.

WJEC Film Studies A2 – FS6: Critical Studies

Sweet Sweetback's Baadasssss Song (1971) could provide an example of either Experimental Film-Making or Shocking Cinema in Section A; Regulation and Censorship or Independent Film and its Audience in Section B; and almost any of the Section C options. Many other black film productions also come under the heading of Independent Film and its Audience while aspects of black cinema may be profitably studied for most of the options in Section C, particularly Performance Studies, for which the Denzel Washington study should prove useful.

CCEA Moving Image Arts – A2 1: Creative Production and Research: Advanced Portfolio

Black cinema could provide case studies for the illustrated essay.

Edexcel BTEC National Diploma Media (Moving Image) – Unit 37: Film Studies

Textual analysis, issues and debates (eg access issues in the mainstream and independent sector), discussion of ideology in film, censorship, genre, auteur theory, institutional context, distribution and exhibition and film audiences, are all areas to which these studies can be applied.

Getting started

At first sight, just by talking about 'black cinema', we are dealing with an unstable and perhaps arbitrary category: to claim that 'black cinema' exists at all seems to suggest some common ground between the very different inhabitants of, say, Dakar, Watts, Trenchtown and Brixton. Even the concept seems suspect, if not actually racist. So we are plunged into controversy from the outset – always a promising basis for study and debate. Teachers may therefore wish to start here, by asking students what they think a 'black' film might be: the definition will probably turn out to be even more elusive than the definition of a 'British' film. Is a black film one made by black filmmakers? Is it one that reflects a black point of view? Or is about the black experience? Or one that features black cast members? According to film actor and erstwhile rapper Ice-T: 'It's a black movie because it's dealing in black dialogue and dialect and expresses culture and how they deal with shit.'

Why study black cinema? For one thing, its history is as interesting as its present. 2002's Oscar ceremony included awards for Best Actor and Best Actress for Denzel Washington and Halle Berry respectively, with an honorary award for Sidney Poitier. However, young audiences who routinely turn out to see films starring Chris Rock, Jada Pinkett Smith, Martin Lawrence or Jamie Foxx may not be aware of the dramatic changes in black screen representation which have taken place in their own lifetimes.

In particular, it is essential to appreciate that from the dawn of cinema until the early 1970s it was taken as read in Hollywood that, with perhaps the single exception of Sidney Poitier, a black actor alone could not 'open' a studio movie. It was not until 1964 that Poitier became the first black actor to win a Best Actor Oscar (for *Lilies of the Field*, Ralph Nelson, US, 1963), and before Gordon Parks directed *The Learning Tree* (US) for Warner Bros. in 1969, no black director had ever been hired by a Hollywood studio. It is important for students to discuss why black people enjoy greater representation today, both on- and off-screen.

Since Hollywood dominates cinema throughout the world it should come as no surprise that it also dominates black screen representation; but the scarcity of black representation elsewhere, including the UK, has had the effect of turning the attention of young black audiences towards America as the place where role models can be found, rather than their own countries. These role models may be Samuel L Jackson or Denzel Washington, but they are equally, if not more, likely to be rap stars like 50 Cent, with all their trappings of new-found wealth, including the latest street fashions, guns, cars, jewellery and a coterie of semi-clad women.

These modern images of blackness are important because they are ubiquitous on music television, and their influence on the fashions of the young of all races worldwide is evident. No study of black screen representation in the cinema or on DVD should ignore the images most often seen by students in a related context. Examination and discussion of these images, along with the assertive and/or aggressive behaviour and language which frequently accompanies them, can then lead to the discovery of where many of them originated – in the blaxploitation films of the 1970s.

African cinema is an essential part of black and World Cinema. Many African films are in French and a variety of indigenous languages such as Wolof. However, the present book concentrates on English-language (Anglophone) films, those which are about the black diaspora, about being a minority in a white-dominated society, or those films with some black element to them whether behind or in front of the camera.

These include films about the black experience in the UK, notably the recent *Bullet Boy* (Saul Dibb, UK, 2004). But even this film proves problematic when defined as a 'black' film since although it was co-scripted by a black woman, it was directed by a white man. Conversely another recent British film, *A Way of Life* (Amma Asante, UK, 2004), written and directed by a black woman, deals with the issue of racism in South Wales, but with a Turkish immigrant as its focus. Does that mean it is in no way an example of black cinema?

Elsewhere there have been some films that qualify as black Anglophone cinema. A very few have been produced in Jamaica, notably *The Harder They Come* (Perry Henzell, Jamaica, 1972), *Smile Orange* (Trevor D Rhone, Jamaica, 1976) and more recently *Dancehall Queen* (Rick Elgood/Don Letts, Jamaica, 1997), *Third World Cop* (Chris Browne, Jamaica, 1999), *Shottas* (Desmond Gumbs, Jamaica/US, 2002), *Rude Boy* (Desmond Gumbs, Jamaica/US) and *One Love* (Rick Elgood/Don Letts, Jamaica/Norway/UK) (both 2003). But as far as the black Caribbean is concerned, most audiences will be more familiar with the 1993 Disney comedy *Cool Runnings* (Jon Turteltaub, US), about the Olympic adventures of the Jamaican bobsleigh team. In Australia and New Zealand, indigenous people often refer to themselves, and are referred to, as black. Should we then regard a Maori film like *Once Were Warriors* (Lee Tamahori, New Zealand, 1994) as an example of black cinema? By now it should be obvious that the category of black film is just as problematic to define as others which students and teachers of film have to grapple with, such as surrealism or independent cinema. This book acknowledges these difficulties and discusses some of the issues connected with them.

Due to the practicalities of teaching the topic, and therefore of obtaining relevant DVDs or videos, this guide will mainly concentrate on the cinema of the USA, and to a lesser extent Britain. The reason for this, and its implications, should be made clear to students. However, those teachers and students with a personal knowledge of and enthusiasm for English-language films from Nigeria, the Caribbean or elsewhere will be able to expand the guide's self-imposed boundaries.

So what other issues are raised by the topic of black cinema? Beginning with the students themselves, young black people are always interested in films featuring people who resemble them. And this is true of all black people (and indeed all people) in all modern societies, since globally Hollywood dominates film and DVD production, distribution and exhibition, and that still very largely means creating and circulating images of white people: the emergence of a substantial 'A' list of black movie stars like Denzel Washington, Halle Berry, Will Smith, Laurence Fishburne and Morgan Freeman has come about only since the 1990s.

Prior to that, and continuing to this day in many instances, is the phenomenon of tokenism – the lone black character in an otherwise all-white cast, usually with no narrative function.[1]

One way of looking at black cinema therefore might be as a form of resistance, explicit or implicit, to white hegemony, whether the films emanate from America, Britain, or anywhere else with a sizeable English-speaking black population. Some sort of equality appears to have been achieved in Hollywood: in the last decade we have seen black stars emerge in roles which might equally have been performed by whites, eg Morgan Freeman in *Se7en* (David Fincher, US, 1995), Wesley Snipes in *Blade* (Stephen Norrington, US, 1998), Laurence Fishburne in *The Matrix* series (Andy and Larry Wachowski, US, 1999–2003), Jamie Foxx in *Collateral* (2004).

Some may see this as evidence that an actor's race is no longer an issue in Hollywood. However, although the idea that the hero of a mainstream Hollywood movie can be black is still very new, who makes and controls these images? This question is about cultural imperialism and ought to extend discussions beyond representation and into questions of minority status, social power and class, access to the media, ideology, art and industry. Minority status in particular deserves our attention, since outside Africa and the Caribbean, black people live in societies in which they are under-represented, both in positions of power and authority, and in the media.

Black audiences complain that stereotypes persist, with too great an emphasis on poverty, drugs and violence. There have been regular calls for more positive images and for lighter material such as romantic and family comedies and middle-class settings. This began to happen with films like *Soul Food* (George Tillman Jr, US, 1997), but even in comedy, the jokes sometimes depend upon black stereotyping which may or may not be intended ironically. In such cases the ethnicity of writer, producer and/or director becomes significant. Robert

---

[1] Andre Braugher in *Poseidon* (Wolfgang Petersen, US, 2006) is one recent example.

Townsend's 1987 comedy *Hollywood Shuffle* makes this point in a scene on the set of a blaxploitation film, in which the writer, producer and director – all white – urge a young black actor to 'be more black'.

This brings us to the issue of representation behind the camera. Black audiences are assiduous filmgoers in the USA, making up 20% of the cinema audience (with only 13% of the population), yet under 5% of Hollywood directors are black. In such circumstances there is sometimes pressure on black directors to 'represent the black community' in their work, thus saddling them with a burden of responsibility in addition to simply making the film. This is a variant on the more usual sense of 'representation' in Film and Media Studies and could be a useful way of illustrating the complexity of the concept.

Film form can also be studied through black cinema: the meaning of genre may be explored through the early 70s' phenomenon of blaxploitation, a cycle of action movies whose influence is still being felt today in the work of directors like Quentin Tarantino and Antoine Fuqua, in countless hip-hop videos, and even in a modern British film like *Rollin' with the Nines* (Julian Gilbey, UK, 2006).

As indicated above, we should be wary of making assumptions about the nature of black cinema: it is very far from being a homogenous category or industry, and it is dangerous to make any hard and fast rules about what might constitute a black film, since a host of exceptions immediately arise.

Like black music, black cinema has shown its ability to cross over into the mainstream and appeal to white audiences. Spike Lee has been perhaps the most successful black American director to achieve this, and in him we have an ideal candidate for auteur study, since he returns frequently to the themes and issues that affect people of his own race. His work raises fundamental questions about whether it is important to sustain a distinctive black voice in the cinema, and hence in other walks of life, or whether integration, or even assimilation, may be preferable – to subsume one's race and traditions into a general modern, multicultural mix.

This guide takes a broadly historical approach to the study of black cinema. The reason for this is the extraordinary degree of social change that continues to the present day and which has deeply affected the way our society deals with blackness and issues of race generally.

Of course, this process continues. Because of the recent increase in the global popularity and hence media visibility of black stars in music, TV and films, students may be inclined to feel that there is nothing left to discuss – that equality has now been achieved, and no barriers remain.[2] Yet they may not be

[2] Equality behind the camera remains elusive. The case brought by the US government against Universal Studios on behalf of sacked black assistant director Frank Davis has yet to come to trial at the time of writing.

aware that slavery existed in Britain until 1834; that it is less than 150 years since it was abolished in the US, less than 40 years since de facto apartheid existed in some southern US states, and little more than a decade since the official end of apartheid in South Africa. According to one reputable source,

> between about 1500 and 1870 it is estimated that at least 12 million African people were forcibly shipped across the Atlantic to work as slaves in the Americas.[3]

The slave trade was an important factor in the growth of British prosperity in the 18th and 19th centuries. Its history is thus as important to white society as it is to black. It is through the study of films, and specifically film representations, that we can come to terms with our joint history. The representations can be traced back to 1915's *The Birth of a Nation* (D W Griffith, US), made when black people were considered incapable of acting in films.

The messages and values of today's commercialised black culture, to which young people are constantly exposed, are equally deserving of examination and discussion. It may be that a process of defamiliarisation would help to situate this modern culture in continuity with the past, and one way to begin would be to engage students in formal deconstructions of moving image texts (eg hip-hop videos) which they may otherwise regard as unproblematic.

Finally, it is important to acknowledge the difficulties which this topic can present in the classroom unless sensitively handled. Teachers unused to conducting discussions of race can sometimes fall foul of stereotyping on the one hand or political correctness on the other, whereas an open-minded, enquiring, research-based approach is probably the one most likely to succeed. At the same time students should be encouraged to explore and acknowledge their own ideological standpoints when discussing issues.

Students who have already studied film for a year, whether in a Film or Media Studies context, are likely to have studied the conventional practices of modern Hollywood and of their own national cinema. The study of black cinema will allow them to look into different contexts of filmmaking – of audience, representation, finance and production, distribution and exhibition. There are also likely to be interesting links with topics such as independent or alternative cinema.

Accordingly, the guide is accompanied by a number of online worksheets which are intended to make the task easier, and which can either be used

---

[3] 'The Portuguese were the first to capture Africans for export during the great Age of Discovery in the 15th century. But by the end of the 18th century they had been joined by the British, Dutch, French and Spanish who were buying almost 100 000 African slaves a year to work on their sugar, cotton, tobacco and rice plantations. Roughly 40% of these Africans were taken to Brazil, 40% to the Caribbean, and the remaining 20% went to the Spanish islands and North America.' http://www.bbc.co.uk/science/genes/dna_detect:ves/african_roots/slaves.shtml

'straight' or adapted as necessary. In addition, further resources in the form of books, websites and DVDs are listed in the References and resources section. These should allow teachers to formulate their own schemes of work and select different texts as desired.

The majority of films recommended for screening, whether as a whole or as extracts, are available on DVD in region 2 (UK/Europe) format. The remainder are only available on VHS in the UK but can be obtained on DVD from the USA (region 1), in which case some possible sources are suggested (see for example http://www.soulcinema.com). For this reason it would be wise to use a multi-region DVD player in the classroom. Where films have not been released on either PAL VHS or DVD, they are not included as recommended resources.

Worksheet 1 begins by opening the debate about the nature of black cinema. Do we know it when we see it? Is any film with a black star automatically a black film, eg Eddie Murphy in *Dr Dolittle* (Betty Thomas, US, 1998)? Students should not be expected to reach firm conclusions yet, but will need to establish some parameters. Some knowledge of the slave trade is essential to developing an understanding of the black/white tensions which have existed for centuries in the developed world. See **Worksheet 2**.

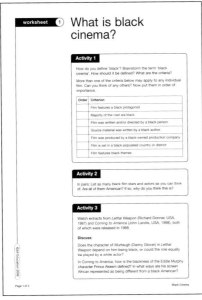

1 of 2 pages

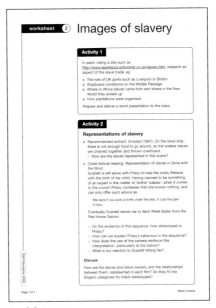

1 of 2 pages

To access student worksheets and other online materials go to *Teaching Black Cinema* at **www.bfi.org.uk/tfms** and enter User name: **blackcine@bfi.org.uk** and Password: **te2007bl**.

This can then lead to consideration of the silent film *The Birth of a Nation*, directed by D W Griffith in 1915. This film is widely considered to be the first masterpiece of cinema, establishing the new medium as the so-called 'seventh art', deserving to be ranked alongside the traditional arts of poetry, dance, music or painting. It established most of the visual and narrative techniques which have since formed the basic grammar of film and is, at nearly three hours long, the longest film ever made at that time. Nevertheless, its content remains extremely controversial.

The writer James Snead considers the film so significant that in his view it was responsible not merely for creating the codes and conventions of cinema, but for helping audiences to regard as normal the racism that existed in the real world. It reportedly made $18 million at the box office, a record which stood for over 20 years. *The Birth of a Nation* is therefore essential viewing for this topic, although a selection of well-chosen extracts would probably be preferable to screening the complete epic. Students may well be shocked by the overtly propagandist nature of the racism. See **Worksheet 3**.

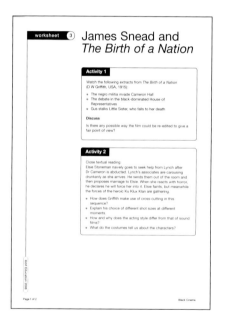

To access student worksheets and other online materials go to *Teaching Black Cinema* at **www.bfi.org.uk/tfms** and enter User name: **blackcine@bfi.org.uk** and Password: **te2007bl**.

While *The Birth of a Nation* may be easily obtained on DVD, it may be harder to find copies of many other silent films, particularly those in which the demeaning black stereotypes typical of the period appear. The career of actor Stepin Fetchit is a case in point (see p48).

● The pleasures of the text

In grappling with the problematics of cinema at A2 Level, there is an occasional tendency among some film academics and teachers to forget that films are made primarily for entertainment. So, with the topic of black cinema, it is sometimes tempting to see only difficult issues and moral dilemmas – whether in the infamous history of slavery and the continuing problem of racism, or in the macho, consumerist street culture of modern hip-hop. But however much teachers may deplore the style or content of certain movies, they were originally produced with the aim of giving pleasure to the audience in return for money. And of course, the commercial imperative has a habit of overriding political correctness. Hence it is important for students to appreciate the formal virtues of *The Birth of a Nation* as well as being struck by its racist agenda; similarly they should be allowed enjoy the outlandish fashions and uninhibited action sequences of *Foxy Brown* (Jack Hill, US, 1974), despite its 'exploitative' elements. In short, the pleasures of the text, whatever its faults and limitations, are a crucial area of film studies.

How to use this guide

The modern context of black cinema is included as a major part of the topic, partly so that students are made aware of its historical links and appreciate the social changes that have taken place, but also because the issues continue to be debated, even as change continues.

Numerous relevant films are mentioned throughout this guide, in the worksheets and on the website, but close textual readings are provided for the following, which are particularly recommended as teaching resources:

The Birth of a Nation	D W Griffith	US	1915
Gone with the Wind	Victor Fleming	US	1939
In the Heat of the Night	Norman Jewison	US	1967
Sweet Sweetback's Baadasssss Song	Melvin Van Peebles	US	1971
Do the Right Thing	Spike Lee	US	1989
The Hurricane	Norman Jewison	US	1999
Bullet Boy	Saul Dibb	UK	2004

In addition, the Filmography indicates which films are used in the worksheets, and provides further and alternative suggestions for films.

This guide is in three sections: Section 1, this Introduction, includes three schemes of work. These may be observed to the letter if necessary, but teachers will usually wish to adapt them to local needs and interests. Section 2 (Background) connects the topic of black cinema to those concepts which students are already likely to have covered earlier in the course – particularly representation, but also audience, narrative, genre, textual analysis, directors and stars. The longest is Section 3 (Case studies) in which both general background and detail is provided on specific examples of black cinema.

The worksheets, which have been written in support of the schemes of work, are available online through the bfi website – www.bfi.org.uk/tfms. Click on the title of the guide then type in the email address **blackcine@bfi.org.uk** Password: **te2007bl**. For the teacher's ease of reference, there is a worksheet for each week in the three schemes of work.

Schemes of work

● Scheme of work 1: Black representation 1915–71

This scheme of work is introductory and historical in approach, designed to start students watching relevant films and get them thinking about what is meant by the term black cinema. They should be encouraged to feel comfortable with the idea that a definition may be difficult to reach, and that there will always be exceptions. Knowing the history and the importance of slavery will contextualise the films viewed, particularly earlier ones such as *The Birth of a Nation* and *Gone with the Wind*. Close textual readings and classroom discussions of film extracts will then enable students to explore the changes that have taken place in screen representation over the years. The difficulties faced by black actors and filmmakers from the 1930s through to the 1950s and 60s are illustrated with reference to such important figures as Paul Robeson, Hattie McDaniel, Sidney Poitier and Dorothy Dandridge.

We then focus on the all-important decade of the 1970s, and in particular on the genre (if it is a genre) of blaxploitation.

The comparisons between the original *Shaft* and the remake will stimulate plenty of initial debate: which film do the students prefer, and why? What cultural changes have taken place in the intervening 30 years, particularly in attitudes towards race and sex? Is violence more acceptable than sex in today's films?

A knowledge of some theoretical writers on race and representation, such as Stuart Hall and bell hooks, will help to underpin students' understanding of the issues. These might include Hall's ideas on representation and cultural identity, and the different ways in which audiences decode texts, and thus the importance of ethnicity. Hall's emphasis on 'otherness' in the racial context is echoed by bell hooks, who has written extensively on matters of gender, race, social class and sexuality.

Aims:

On completing this unit, students should be able to:

- Understand what might be considered black cinema and what issues any possible definitions might raise
- Make connections between the themes of this study and the concept of screen representation as a whole
- Understand the genre of blaxploitation and its origins.

Outcomes:

Students will:

- Develop their skills of textual analysis by comparing films from different eras
- Broaden their understanding of film representation, institutions and audiences beyond what they learned at AS Level
- Increase their knowledge of social change and cultural history in film.

Week 1 What is black cinema?

- Brainstorm the term 'black cinema'. How should it be defined? What are the criteria?
- Pair activity: List as many black film stars as you can. Are all of them American? If so, why do you think this is?
- Watch extracts from *Lethal Weapon* (1987) and *Coming to America* (1988)
- Discussion: Does the character of Murtaugh (Danny Glover) in *Lethal Weapon* depend on him being black or could the role equally be played by a white actor?
- In *Coming to America*, how is the blackness of the Eddie Murphy character Prince Akeem defined? In what ways are his screen African represented as being different from a black American?
- Pair activity: Think of four other films featuring black actors, two in which the ethnicity of the characters seems to be important to the role, and two in which it does not. How and why do these differences exist?
- Read about Donald Bogle's five black stereotypes. What examples of these stereotypes have you noticed in recent films?

Week 2 Images of slavery

- Pair activity: Research an aspect of the slave trade
- Prepare and deliver short presentation to the class
- Recommended extract: *Amistad* (1997). How are the slaves represented in the selected scene?
- Close textual reading: Representation of slaves in *Gone with the Wind* (1939)
- Discussion: How are the slaves and slave-owners, and the relationships between them, represented in each film? Do they fit into Bogle's categories for black stereotypes?

Week 3 James Snead and *The Birth of a Nation* (1915)

- Recommended extract: *The Birth of a Nation*
- Discussion: Is there any possible way the film could be re-edited to give a fair point of view?
- Close textual reading
- Read the reactions of critic James Snead
- Consider what 'nostalgic' effects the film might have had on American audiences of the time; what the 'extra-cinematic codes' might be; whether the myths Snead describes remain with us today.

Week 4 The 1930s: From Stepin Fetchit to Paul Robeson

- Pair activity: Research the lives and careers of such actors as Stepin Fetchit, Bill 'Bojangles' Robinson, Louise Beavers, Eddie 'Rochester' Anderson, Willie 'Sleep'n'Eat' Best, Fredi Washington, Hattie McDaniel, and Butterfly McQueen, and such pioneer filmmakers as William Foster and Oscar Micheaux. Answer the questions on **Worksheet 4** and feed back to the rest of the group
- Recommended extracts: *Here I Stand* (1999), a documentary about the life of Paul Robeson and extracts from his films *Song of Freedom* (1936) and *Big Fella* (1937)
- Using **Worksheet 4**'s questions as prompts, research his life
- Why did Robeson find a more sympathetic film audience in the UK than in his own country?

Week 5 The 1950s: Sidney Poitier and Dorothy Dandridge

- Research 'Jim Crow' laws; the Montgomery Bus Boycott; the Freedom Riders; the March on Washington
- Recommended extract: The Sidney Poitier/Tony Curtis film *The Defiant Ones* (1958). What messages and values do you think the film is trying to convey?
- Close textual reading: *In the Heat of the Night* (1967)
- Activity: Construct a profile of Sidney Poitier's star persona
- Alternative/additional activity: Using the criteria on **Worksheet 5** (and substituting 'femininity' for 'masculinity'), construct a profile of Dorothy Dandridge's career. Do you see any parallels with the screen persona of Halle Berry?

Week 6 The 1970s: Blaxploitation and the new assertive black man

- Recommended extracts: *Shaft* (2000) and the original *Shaft*, released in 1971
- Answer the questions on **Worksheet 6**
- What do you consider to be the codes and conventions of blaxploitation? Take into account such generic codes as typical themes, stock characters, stock plots, settings, costumes and soundtracks

- While studying blaxploitation in future lessons, consider whether it is a real genre, or just a loose category.

Week 7 *Sweet Sweetback's Baadasssss Song* (1971)
- Read the case study notes
- Watch the film and answer the questions on style, theme and genre in **Worksheet 7**
- Close textual reading.

● Scheme of work 2: Blaxploitation, Spike Lee and the new black stars

This scheme of work links with the previous one in examining the ways in which blaxploitation appears to have influenced subsequent filmmakers and movements, especially the black new wave of the early 1990s. It also aims to establish a social link between the new assertiveness of black people in 1970s' America with the simultaneous advent of Black Power and the wider social movement of 'black is beautiful', with its funky music, 'natural' hairstyles and flamboyant African-style fashions.

From this point we begin to look at broader issues of film industry practice, the importance of distribution and exhibition to black film, the representation of women, and the crucial position occupied by the new black stars who began to appear in the early 1990s – in this case, Denzel Washington. We also examine the early 1990s boom in black filmmaking, which was sparked in the late 80s by the provocative films of Spike Lee.

Aims:
On completing this unit, students should be able to:
- Assess blaxploitation's influences and its effects on modern cinema as well as in an industrial and a broader social context
- Consider the representation of women in black cinema
- Assess the importance of the black new wave, and the work of an iconic director (Spike Lee) and star (Denzel Washington).

Outcomes:
Students will:
- Extend their understanding of the changing nature of black screen representation over time, including the issue of stereotyping
- Further develop the ability to identify and discuss genre codes and conventions
- Examine and debate the auteurist credentials of Spike Lee
- Identify the characteristics of independent production and the modes of alternative, avant-garde and political cinema.

Week 1 The legacy of blaxploitation

- **Worksheet 8**
- Research: The Black Power movement. What were its aims and who were its leading figures? Can you see its influence on blaxploitation films?
- Recommended extract: The documentary *Baadasssss Cinema: A Bold Look At 70s' Blaxploitation Films* (2002)
- Discussion: What social role do you think the blaxploitation films played in the 1970s? How and why did the genre die out so quickly? Take into account the messages and values typical of the genre, industry factors (eg producers and directors, ownership and control of studios), as well as the social context of the time
- Recommended extracts: *Original Gangstas* (1996) and *Undercover Brother* (2002)
- Consider the influence of 1970s' blaxploitation cinema on hip-hop and on more recent films.

Week 2 Distribution and exhibition

- Research: Using <u>imdb.com</u>, find out which were the most commercially successful of the blaxploitation films. Why do you think these succeeded where others failed?
- **Worksheet 9:** Programme a local season of blaxploitation films and plan the marketing. This includes identifying the target audience, writing a promotional leaflet, designing a poster, booking paid advertising, arranging publicity and defending the films in the face of local criticism. Present your plan to the group
- Extension activity: *Hitch* (2005) poster analysis.

Week 3 Women in black cinema

- **Worksheet 10**
- Discussion: Laura Mulvey's *Visual Pleasure and Narrative Cinema* (1975)
- Recommended extract: The scene from *Crash* (2005) in which the characters played by Terrence Howard (Cameron) and Thandie Newton (Christine) are harassed by policeman Matt Dillon (John Ryan). What are our responses to this scene, bearing in mind Mulvey's ideas?
- Recommended extract: The title sequence from *Foxy Brown* (1974). Is Pam Grier being objectified, in Mulvey's sense of the term? Or are there other ways in which we might respond to the sequence?
- Research: How many women directors are working in Hollywood today and how many of them are black?
- Discussion: Is it important that women in general, and black women in particular, should direct movies, and if so, why?

Week 4 Spike Lee and the concept of the independent filmmaker

- Recommended extract: *Malcolm X* (1992)
- Read the quotations from Malcolm X and Martin Luther King from the end of *Do the Right Thing* (1989)
- Discussion: How do the quotations clarify the dilemma facing black people in America? Might this dilemma extend to black and other minorities in white-dominated societies beyond the USA?
- Research: Find more quotations to illustrate the differences in approach between the two leaders
- Research: Read pp45–78 of John Pierson's book *Spike, Mike, Slackers & Dykes* (Faber, 1997)
- Consider the questions in **Worksheet 11**.

Week 5 Spike Lee and auteurism

- **Worksheet 12**
- Recommended extract: *Do the Right Thing*
- Close textual reading
- Recommended extracts: From a wide variety of Spike Lee films
- Discussion: If Spike Lee is indeed an auteur, which kind is he? In four groups, list some common characteristics in his films. Each group should look at a different area of auteurist criticism
- Present your findings to the class.

Week 6 The black new wave

- Recommended extracts: *Fresh* (1994) and *Boyz N the Hood* (1991)
- Answer the questions on narrative and representation in **Worksheet 13**.

Week 7 Star study: Denzel Washington

- Group activity: Having watched extracts from a number of Denzel Washington films, piece together a 300-word star profile of Washington as an actor. Start with his screen persona, giving actual examples from the films
- Each group should then feed back to the class
- Research: Find out which of Denzel Washington's movies has made the most money. Do the findings shed any new light on our understanding of his persona?
- Close textual reading: *The Hurricane* (1999)
- Activity: Carry out a commutation test on the central character. In this case, what differences would occur if a particular white actor (say, Tom Hanks or Tom Cruise) took on the role played by Denzel Washington?

● Scheme of work 3: Black cinema today

The third and final scheme of work continues to examine some of the broader aspects of modern black cinema, such as arthouse films and recent comedy successes like *Big Momma's House* (2000) and *Soul Plane* (2004). We also explore the enormous influence of hip-hop and the connected issues of gender representation. The scheme of work ends by investigating some relevant examples of British cinema, past and present. Beginning with the British Empire, we move on to look at black British cinema in the 21st century, how it reflects our cultural attitudes and concerns, and whether it has a future.

Students will be able to bring their own knowledge to bear on many of these topics, since they are likely to be familiar with the films and stars. It is therefore important for teachers to ensure that critical focus is maintained by referring back regularly to earlier films and social themes, and by encouraging students to make connections. In particular, the nature and origins of 'gangsta' culture and the reasons for its worldwide popularity should be debated.

This should lead to discussions about the future of black filmmaking outside the USA, what it might consist of, and how distinctive it should be. The construction and representation of personal identity and nationhood, as well as racial difference, are all likely to be issues in these debates. There are also comparisons to be made with black representation in films normally considered as World Cinema, eg *La Haine* (1995), *Once Were Warriors* (1994).

Aims:
On completing this unit, students should be able to:
● Understand modern black cinema within its historical context
● Understand issues and debates around black representation today
● Make informed assessments of the current state and influence of black cinema, and of its possible futures.

Outcomes:
Students will:
● Broaden their knowledge of film genre
● Gain a clearer understanding of concepts and debates relating to gender, personal identity, ethnicity and nationhood
● Recognise the main issues facing modern British black filmmakers and actors, linking these with studies of production, distribution and exhibition, and the film audience.

Week 1 Black arthouse
● Define 'arthouse', both in terms of the kind of films and their audience
● Why is there often an overlap between arthouse films and independent cinema?

- Recommended extracts: *To Sleep with Anger* (1990) and *Daughters of the Dust* (1991)
- Why might we designate them 'arthouse'?
- Examine the extras on the DVD of *George Washington* (2000), then answer the questions in **Worksheet 15**
- Research: How did the film perform at the box office?

Week 2 Hip-hop culture on screen

- **Worksheet 16**
- What black music stars have appeared in recent films, and in what kind of roles?
- Activity: Students should bring in their favourite hip-hop videos and make short presentations about them, deconstructing the representations in the light of studies carried out so far, particularly regarding representations of masculinity, women and gangsta culture, as well as the influence of blaxploitation
- Discussion: What does the popularity of hip-hop and its associated imagery say about modern street culture (eg 'bling', guns, drugs)? Is there any indication of moral panic in the media regarding their supposed bad influence on young people? (Remember that the 'effects' theory usually forms part of this discussion)
- What different reactions do class members have to these videos?

Week 3 Comedy in black cinema*

- Discussion: Are there any genre conventions of comedy in black cinema beyond those of comedy films in general?
- Recommended extracts: *Soul Plane* and *Big Momma's House*
- Discussion: Consider the questions in **Worksheet 17**
- Essay question: Outline what you consider to be the main issues of spectatorship in *Soul Plane* and *Big Momma's House*, and if possible in any other comedy films you have seen with a largely black cast and/or director.

  * Be aware that the term 'black comedy' has a specific and separate meaning from 'funny black films'. For the sake of clarity, try to avoid using 'black comedy' except in its original sense.

Week 4 Sex and romance

- Discussion: Consider the questions raised in **Worksheet 18**
- Recommended extract: *Jungle Fever* (1991) from the scene with Drew and her friends, just after she has thrown Flipper out, through to his attempt at reconciliation. Does the extract confirm or cast doubt on the conclusions reached previously? What other issues are raised by the extract?

- Recommended extract: *Waiting to Exhale* (1995). Do the female characters survive the Joanna Russ test? Could the film have been made by a white director?
- Recommended extract: Spike Lee's first film *She's Gotta Have It* (1986)
- Consider the questions in **Worksheet 18**.

Week 5 Black cinema in the UK

- Research: The British Empire. Which modern countries were once British colonies?
- Research: Black British cinema up to 1990. What films were made, and what were they about?
- Recommended extract: The final 15 minutes (or more) of *Zulu* (1964), then answer the questions in **Worksheet 19**
- Recommended extracts: *Pressure* (1976) and the whole of *Burning an Illusion* (1981)
- Discussion: Consider the issues raised in **Worksheet 19**.

Week 6 Modern black British Cinema

- Recommended extracts: To familiarise yourself with British 'kitchen-sink' movies, watch brief extracts from one or two classics such as *Saturday Night and Sunday Morning* (1960), *Kes* (1969), *Raining Stones* (1993) or *Vera Drake* (2004).
- Recommended extracts: *A Way of Life* (2004) and *Bullet Boy* (2004). Do you see parallels in the way the newer films have been directed? Considering such elements as lighting, sound, camerawork, décor, performance, why exactly might we categorise them as examples of realist cinema?
- Consider the comment from the imdb.com message board in **Worksheet 20**. Do you agree with it?
- Close textual reading: *Bullet Boy*.

Week 7 The future of black cinema

- Activity: Read the background information in **Worksheet 21**. What additional information can you discover about this film's production, distribution and exhibition history? Was the marketing strategy the correct one for a film of this type? Justify your comments. What did reviewers and audience members say about it?
- Activity: In pairs or small groups, devise a black-oriented British film which might stand a better chance of success in the cinema than *Rollin' with the Nines* (2006). (Also consider 'back-end' and overseas earnings potential). Pitch your idea to the group
- Discussion: Is the concept of black cinema out of date in a multicultural world?
- Essay title: Can black cinema survive in the 21st century?

2

Background

Introduction

By now most teachers will appreciate that the study of black cinema can reveal a rich – in some ways alternative – seam of cultural history leading right up to the present. This in turn may encourage new ways of seeing the world. But we should not try to pigeonhole black cinema or see it as some kind of discrete entity: it is not a genre, although it may be possible to identify some recurring characteristics. It is more a case of seeing parallels in aspects of black cinema with certain movements and styles across cinema as a whole. Similarly, studying black cinema helps to illustrate the key terms and concepts which underlie Film and Media Studies. Finally, it aids students' broader education, forming links with other subjects they may be taking.

One illustration of this last point is the issue of politics and power in the modern world. Hollywood's domination of black representation has had the effect of positioning black people as a global minority, without power or influence to change things. Some may regard this as a contentious statement. In fact, wherever we look, controversy lurks, which means that politics (in the broad sense) is never far away.

When we consider Africa and the Caribbean, for example, it might be said that since black people are in the majority, and no longer in thrall to colonial masters, they run their own affairs. Yet this assertion would be contested by those who maintain that nation states are of no importance in a 'globalised' world controlled by the G8 and its manifestations: the UN Security Council, the World Bank, the International Monetary Fund and the World Trade Organisation, not to mention business conglomerates like Microsoft, Coca-Cola, Nike and Disney.

Discussing such issues may, on the face of it, appear to be rather beyond the scope of the A Level Film or Media Studies specifications, but when examined alongside other academic disciplines such as Politics, History or Economics, they can allow students to form important links, to see issues in the round.

Within the parameters of Film and Media Studies, examining the social and political aspects of black cinema can supply the sort of cultural contexts frustratingly absent in some student essays. In such cases, film appears to exist in a vacuum, divorced from everyday life. But it would be difficult, for instance, to understand *The Defiant Ones* (Stanley Kramer, US, 1958) with no knowledge of the Civil Rights movement in the US and everything that led up to it. See **Worksheet 5.**

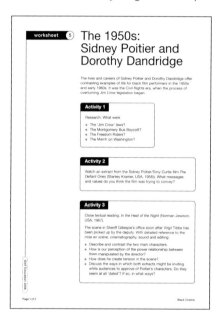

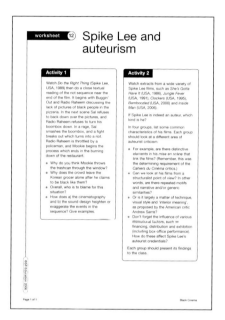

To access student worksheets and other online materials go to *Teaching Black Cinema* at **www.bfi.org.uk/tfms** and enter User name: **blackcine@bfi.org.uk** and Password: **te2007bl**.

The rage that drives the rioters in *Do the Right Thing* (Spike Lee, US, 1989) likewise could seem baffling: How could an argument over photographs in a pizza restaurant lead to this? Until we know the context of black cultural and economic marginalisation, we might be forgiven for thinking that the characters are merely perverse or perhaps just unruly by nature. See **Worksheet 12.**

As mentioned above, we can also use black cinema to learn more about the key concepts of cinema as a whole. The following section begins by suggesting some categories in which we might be able to place types of black cinema. The section then shows how certain key concepts can be understood in relation to it.

Categories of cinema

See Black cinema: A brief timeline of key moments, which provides a broad context for this section.

● African cinema

As stated in Section 1, it is not the intention of the present guide to cover African cinema, nor can we entirely ignore it when discussing black cinema. A case in point is 'Nollywood' – the name given to the popular and presently burgeoning Nigerian film industry, which produces 2,000 films a year in the Yoruba, Ibo and English languages, and is now reckoned to be the third largest film industry in the world. Ultra-low budgets are possible for these films, which are shot on digital video and distributed on VCD to expatriate communities throughout the world. Categorisation of these films can be difficult: for instance, the comedy *Osuofia in London* (Kingsley Ogoro, Nigeria, 2003) features several British actors and half of it was shot in England.

Two Francophone directors are pre-eminent among living African filmmakers whose work is known in the West – Senegal's Ousmane Sembène and Souleymane Cissé from Mali.[4] Both are concerned with the African experience of post-colonialism but also with what it means to be African in the modern (and postmodern) world. Many of the films put a particular value on the community rather than the individual, and reflect attitudes to time and space that are very distinct from those of the developed world. Outside Africa these films tend to appear in the category of art cinema, to the extent that they are exhibited, if at all, in arthouse cinemas and at film festivals rather than in mainstream theatres. It may well be worthwhile asking your students whether they would be interested in studying some of the key films. For teachers wishing to find out about African cinema, some useful resources are included at the end of this guide. Unfortunately, few non-Nollywood films are currently available on DVD.

● Black American cinema

Since black American cinema encompasses such a range of films, it will be more convenient to subdivide it into mainstream Hollywood, black independent cinema, blaxploitation and black art films. There are of course overlaps between these categories.

Mainstream Hollywood

Today's students take for granted that a film star can be black, since this has been the case for as long as they can remember. However, those with slightly longer memories will know that the present situation is the result of a revolution in black screen representation since the early 1990s.

---

[4] Sembène's *Moolaadé* (2004) is a focus film option in WJEC's Film Studies 2007–8 specification, paper FS5 (World Cinema).

Black independent cinema

Before embarking on any research, it might be useful for students to suggest what a truly independent black cinema might look like.

Spike Lee is the doyen of independent black filmmakers (see Case study 4), but perhaps the most clear-cut examples of black independent cinema were produced in the silent era. Directors William Foster and Oscar Micheaux are the most striking examples. Under Jim Crow laws, the only way for black people to find work in the film industry or even go the cinema was to create their own industry.[5] Micheaux and others made 'race films' exclusively for black audiences, who watched them in black cinemas, many of which were black-owned. Although these films are hard to find today, students may well find it rewarding to research this phenomenon which (apart from Micheaux's company) did not survive the Wall Street Crash (1929). See **Worksheet 4.**

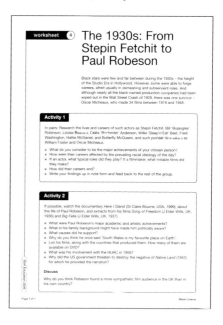

To access student worksheets and other online materials go to *Teaching Black Cinema* at **www.bfi.org.uk/tfms** and enter User name: **blackcine@bfi.org.uk** and Password: **te2007bl**.

Blaxploitation

The nearest black cinema subsequently came to a degree of ownership and control was during the brief heyday of blaxploitation in the early 1970s when films not only starred black actors but some had black directors and producers. Melvin Van Peebles' *Sweet Sweetback's Baadasssss Song* (US, 1971) and *Superfly* (Gordon Parks Jr, US, 1972), financed by a consortium of Harlem businesses, are perhaps the most notable examples. The films of actor-director-producer Fred Williamson provide more. However, distribution and exhibition were by then firmly in the hands of whites.

---

[5] 'Jim Crow' laws were those passed by individual states in the teeth of the equality legislation enacted by the federal government in the aftermath of the Civil War. Segregation of blacks and whites was imposed in most areas of life, including housing, education, transport and the right to vote. 'Jim Crow' existed in some southern states until the mid-1960s.

Blaxploitation deserves a category of its own because it marked a major cultural shift which paved the way for today's much improved levels of representation for black people on both sides of the camera. Its importance for black cinema was that for the first time since the 1920s it enabled black directors to work with black actors and enjoy the commercial backing necessary for success.

As with black cinema as a whole, discussion needs to take place about whether there is really any coherent group of films which can be termed blaxploitation. Certainly, certain codes and conventions will be instantly recognisable to many students for the style borrowed from it by 1990s' 'hood' and 'gangsta' movies, and by the videos of rap artists from the same era. Spotting these influences would be an interesting and relevant activity for students.

The topic may prove contentious, as it certainly was during the period in question. It should ask who is the exploiter and who, if anyone, is being exploited – the audience, the female characters, or black people as a whole through a new set of stereotypes, or perhaps all of the above? The experience of having watched earlier films, in which the black characters are generally quiescent, should provide a useful contrast with the far more assertive protagonists of blaxploitation.

Blaxploitation's most well-known films are the original version of *Shaft* (Gordon Parks Jr, US, 1971), and *Superfly* (1972), although the cycle was kick-started by *Sweet Sweetback's Baadasssss Song*. See **Worksheets 6 and 7**. Some 200 films have been identified as belonging to this category, yet it was short-

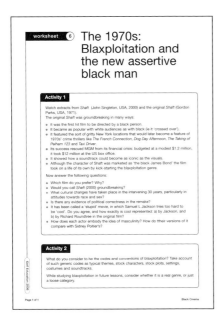

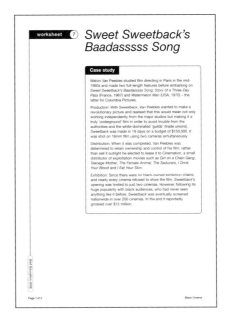

lived. By the mid-1970s it was coming to an end, although there have since been several revivals and parodies such as *I'm Gonna Git You Sucka* (Keenen Ivory Wayans, US, 1988), *Dead Presidents* (Albert Hughes/Allen Hughes, US, 1995), *Original Gangstas* (Larry Cohen, US, 1996) and *Undercover Brother* (Malcolm D Lee, US, 2002). **See Worksheet 8**.

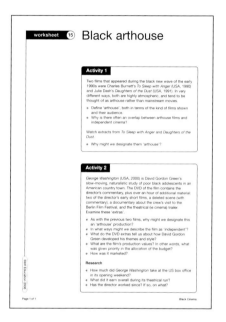

To access student worksheets and other online materials go to *Teaching Black Cinema* at **www.bfi.org.uk/tfms** and enter User name: **blackcine@bfi.org.uk** and Password: **te2007bl**.

The black art film

An art film is generally non-commercial, independently made, employing innovative, perhaps experimental, techniques, and appealing to educated niche audiences. The work of Charles Burnett and Julie Dash could be said to fall into this category, as could white director David Gordon Green's *George Washington* (US, 2000). See **Worksheet 15**.

● **Black British cinema**

Few films have been made about the experience of being black in Britain, and fewer still have received cinema exhibition. Those that have been made tend to fall into three categories: films about the British Empire, films about recent immigrants to the UK and films about alienated black youth. And just as black American cinema has long been overshadowed by the legacy of slavery, many British black representations are haunted by memories of the British Empire. It would be worth checking early on in the teaching process how aware students are of that empire which, as the British used to be reminded on a regular basis, was the largest the world had ever seen.

A number of recent British films have focused on the plight of asylum seekers and recent immigrants to the UK from all over the world, not only the former colonies. In *Dirty Pretty Things* (Stephen Frears, UK, 2002), for example, London-born Chiwetel Ejiofor plays a Nigerian doctor reduced to working illegally in a London hotel.

Films about the Empire date back at least to the 1930s when American singing star Paul Robeson appeared as a succession of Africans in such British productions as *Sanders of the River* (Zoltan Korda, UK, 1935), *Song of Freedom* (J Elder Wills, UK, 1936) and *Jericho* (Thornton Freeland, UK, 1937).

Basil Dearden's *Sapphire* (UK, 1959) focuses on racism and bigotry towards newly arrived Caribbean immigrants. *Flame in the Streets* (Roy Ward Baker, UK, 1961) examines the issue of prejudice in the workplace while *A Taste of Honey* (Tony Richardson, UK, 1961) sees a young woman falling pregnant after a fling with a black sailor. John Boorman's *Leo the Last* (UK, 1969) is set in black Notting Hill. *Pressure* (UK, 1975) – directed by Trinidad-born Horace Ové and therefore often thought of as the first truly black British film – shows in an edgy documentary style how difficult it was for British-born black youths to find work. *Black Joy* (Anthony Simmons, UK, 1977) is a comedy about a naive immigrant from Guyana experiencing life in the Brixton ghetto, while *Babylon* (Franco Rosso, UK, 1980) is the story of an alienated young Rastafarian trying to make a name for himself with his reggae sound system.

In the 1980s political polarisation brought about by a radical Conservative government led to a number of films from new black directors, including *Burning an Illusion* (Menelik Shabazz, UK, 1981) and *Handsworth Songs* (John Akomfrah, UK, 1986). Ové's cricket drama *Playing Away* (UK/US) also appeared that year. Isaac Julien's *Young Soul Rebels* (UK/France/ Germany/Spain, 1991) tackles gay as well as racial themes. Female director Ngozi Onwurah's *Welcome II the Terrordome* (UK, 1995) puts forward a science-fiction future world in which all black people have been confined to a giant ghetto. *Babymother* (Julian Henriques, UK, 1998) is a musical set in the dancehall culture of London's Harlesden. *Emotional Backgammon* (Leon Herbert, UK, 2003) is a drama about the battle of the sexes. However, none of these films succeeded in finding an audience at the box office.

In recent years greater cultural integration has become a feature of British society. 2004 saw the release of two films with black involvement, both of which were superior in almost every way to any that had gone before. *A Way of Life* (2004) was made by a black woman about white people living in South

Wales while *Bullet Boy* (2004) was directed by a white man about young black men in East London. (See **Worksheet 20** p74.) Comparisons between these films and American productions like *American History X* (Tony Kaye, US, 1998) and *Fresh* (Boaz Yakin, US, 1994) could help students to explore cultural differences between the two countries as well as differing attitudes to race.

Key terms and concepts

In any discussion of the media we may usefully invoke the 'media concepts triangle', which reminds teachers and students of the three interconnected aspects of a) the text itself, b) the industry or institution which produced it and c) its audience. We can find illustrations of these relationships through the study of black cinema.

● The text

The key to textual analysis is not only a command of the specialist vocabulary but also the ability to use it as a set of tools to crack open the text, revealing its underlying messages and values. Representation is perhaps the easiest place to start. Stuart Hall (1997) argues that since there is no biological difference between the races, ideas of racial difference are entirely cultural, and therefore have to be examined using semiotics:

> The very obviousness of the visibility of race convinces me that it functions as a signifying system, as a text we can read.

In other words, representations are central to discussions of race because

> reality does not exist outside the process of representation.[6]

In 'Taking Popular Television Seriously' (1985), Richard Dyer proposes four different connotations for this concept, all of which are pertinent to black cinema:

1. Representation as a re-presentation of reality – how a text makes sense of the world;
2. Representation as 'being typical of ...' An unavoidable form of cultural shorthand that can also create stereotyping;
3. Representation 'in the sense of speaking for and on behalf of ...' Whose values and ideas are really being expressed in the text?
4. Representation as in 'What does this represent to me personally?' In other words, personal interpretation of the text.

We could take as an example Spike Lee's *Do the Right Thing*:

---

[6] From the video *Race, the Floating Signifier* (1997).

1. What do the story and the characters in this film suggest to us about American society? Let's not worry about its accuracy or fairness – it was not possible for Spike Lee to create a perfect reflection of reality, and in any case we have no way of knowing whether it was 'true' at the time it was made. Instead we need to consider the issues raised by the fictional personalities and events. What does the film have to say about, for example, the relationship – personal and economic – between its Italians and its blacks?

2. We could now move on to examine the two cultures and what the film has to say about each of them. Are the Italians represented as being typical of whites or of Italians specifically? How might they and the black characters be seen to contribute to the problem through their different behaviour and traditions, for example in attitudes towards work and ownership?

3. The film is overt in its political references at the end when quotations from Malcolm X and Martin Luther King scroll up the screen. Who in the film could be seen as representative of these opposing points of view, and does Spike Lee give any hint of his own position on the issues? How far, in a broader sense, can he be described as representing black America?[7]

4. How do we relate to the story as individual audience members? In AS Film Studies students are actively encouraged to focus on their individual response to films; in other words to explain how and why they react to what they see and hear, without necessarily the aid of theory or suggestions from the teacher. In the case of *Do the Right Thing*, do we feel that either side in the conflict is to blame? If so, why?

See **Worksheet 12** (p26).

● Industry/institution

We are fortunate to be working as Film and Media Studies teachers at a time when both the internet and DVD 'extras' exist to give us an insight into the previously closed world of the film industry. The Internet Movie Database (www.imdb.com) is a goldmine of information on films, actors, filmmakers, distributors and box-office receipts, complete with dialogue quotes, shooting locations, trailers, posters, publicity stills, press reviews and audience opinions. DVDs contain trailers, behind-the-scenes footage, alternative endings, cast and crew interviews, directors' commentaries, biographies and sometimes even previous work by the same director. Posters and trailers reveal the genre and target market for most films.

---

[7] The issue is well expressed by Bogle (2003): 'Black movies – particularly those popular ones with built-in commercial appeal – remain so few and far between that each one is viewed almost as if it were the only black film ever made, as if it should satisfy all our needs, as if summed up in total black America's frame of mind.'

George Washington (2000) is a slow-moving, naturalistic study of poor black adolescents in an American country town. On the DVD of the film, the director's commentary can be switched on or off during the playing of the film. The DVD also contains over an hour of additional material: two of the director's early short films, a deleted scene (with commentary), a documentary about the crew's visit to the Berlin Film Festival, and the theatrical (ie cinema) trailer.

Why do we need all this information? The film industry is divided into production, distribution and exhibition, and each stage of making, marketing and showing a film to the public can present both problems and opportunities. *George Washington* was made and distributed independently from the Hollywood system. Its 25-year-old white director David Gordon Green developed his themes gradually through his early work at the North Carolina School of the Arts, as we learn from watching the two shorts on the DVD. He spent his restricted budget not on stars or special effects but on obtaining the best possible quality sound and vision, including the use of anamorphic lenses to give the film the lush, cinematic 1970s' look Green wanted.

All this tells us a great deal about how and why the film turned out the way it did. The footage taken at the film festival gives an insight into how the film was marketed overseas to its arthouse audience. Even the fact that in the UK it was released on DVD by the British Film Institute, rather than, say, Buena Vista, suggests to us that it is not a mainstream Hollywood movie.

As far as exhibition is concerned, from imdb.com we learn that the film opened on five screens in the USA and earned the princely sum of $13,335 at the box office on its opening weekend. By the end of its theatrical run that figure stood at $241,816. However, in this case no figures are supplied for original budget or subsequent DVD sales or overseas box-office receipts. What we do know is that today the 'back end' – mainly DVD but also sales of TV and other ancillary rights – is the main source of revenue for the film industry, rather than sales of cinema tickets. And of course the critical acclaim the film received should have enabled Green to raise a larger budget for his next production. See **Worksheet 15** (p30).

● Audience

Our students' interest in film and media stems from their roles as audience members, however they may eventually progress, whether as film scholars or even as producers in their own right. Finding out about their viewing knowledge, habits and preferences is therefore an essential starting point for any film or media topic. In researching this book I discussed with a number of young black people the sort of films they enjoy and their context of viewing, and this contributed greatly to my understanding – both of their behaviour as a film audience and of the topic as a whole. What do they watch and enjoy? Do they visit the cinema or prefer DVDs? Where do they find the films they like, especially those which do not receive theatrical release? Do they watch pirate copies? How important is the role of word of mouth, advertising or the internet in deciding what films they see?

For example, from my own small sample it seems that most young black Londoners watch their films on DVD rather than go to the cinema.[8] They often obtain them not through conventional retailers but from each other, from specialist black music shops, from street markets, and so on.

Audiences are not usually as easy to categorise as we might think. Black audiences watch a lot of mainstream Hollywood cinema, and some neither know nor care about black films. Conversely a black filmmaker like Spike Lee is of great interest to many white film fans due to the sheer power and passion of his films, his offbeat subject matter and his command of cinematic technique.

It is important to consider in what ways a particular audience is targeted by the producers of films. The Will Smith romantic comedy *Hitch* (Andy Tennant, US, 2005) was clearly targeted at a mainstream multiplex audience, distributed as it was by Columbia in the USA and by Columbia-Tristar and Sony internationally. Neither the trailer nor the poster plays up the star's ethnicity. The poster features a relaxed and smiling Smith pictured full-length, looking straight at the camera, and casually dressed, with the tag-line 'The cure for the common man'. This suggests that the film depends heavily on its star, who is the only cast member with above-the-title billing.

'The common man' reinforces the impression that here is a movie intended for the masses. See **Worksheet 9**.

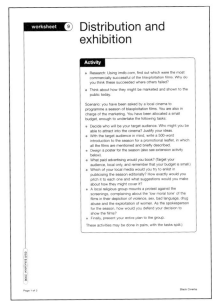

To access student worksheets and other online materials go to *Teaching Black Cinema* at **www.bfi.org.uk/tfms** and enter User name: **blackcine@bfi.org.uk** and Password: **te2007bl**.

---

[8] British writer and director Amma Asante claims that audiences who saw her film *A Way of Life* on the big screen experienced a stronger emotional reaction than those who watched it on DVD.

The audience's familiarity with Will Smith's previous films and TV series and his established screen persona are crucial to the success of *Hitch*. Although Smith has appeared in straight drama – eg *Six Degrees of Separation* (Fred Schepisi, US, 1993); *Enemy of the State* (Tony Scott, US, 1998); *I, Robot* (Alex Proyas, US, 2004) – we strongly suspect that the genre of *Hitch* will be comedy. Viewing the trailer not only confirms this suspicion but also identifies it more specifically as a romantic comedy.

Students will be able to study promotional material for other films and draw reasoned conclusions about the target audience – in terms of age, gender, social class, race – from the available evidence.

We also need to consider audience reaction, over and above the film's popularity as indicated by its profitability. Once again imdb.com can help: attached to each film are message boards promoting and debating a whole range of opinions about it. While most subjects raised by viewers of *Hitch* generated four or five responses, one headed 'Race question' stimulated 25. The original message concerned Hollywood's supposed inability to tolerate mixed-race relationships. One reply was

> I don't think anything about race when watching a movie. I'm above that. It's a movie. Grow up and get over it.

Another commented:

> Imagine Will Smith and let's say Sandra Bullock as the lead female. You may not be aware of it, but the average person will have at least a slight discomfort with that romantic link deep inside them.

● Textual analysis

The ability to analyse media texts is fundamental to teaching the subject and, for students, to the successful completion of coursework and to passing exams. WJEC's AS Film Studies coursework requires students to write two close textual analyses, one on narrative and genre (the 'macro' elements of a film text), and the other on any combination of *mise en scène*, performance, cinematography, sound and editing (the 'micro' elements). The development of these skills is essential in most areas of the A2 syllabus. Every Media Studies AS and A Level syllabus also requires students to demonstrate their ability to analyse texts – often 'unseen'. These texts are quite likely to be film trailers or extracts.

As mentioned above, the students will need to be equipped with a command of the specialist vocabulary and the 'tools' to reveal a range of possible meanings, messages and values in the text. Representation has already been discussed, but we should now consider how analysis can be carried out in practice, with reference to black cinema texts.

● Narrative

There is no single narrative style specific to black cinema. However, the theme of a film can sometimes dictate its narrative structure. Most films follow the simple formula of exposition and conflict, development, climax and resolution. Unless a sequel is planned (or the film is arthouse) there will usually be total closure: we expect to know the fate of each character, the outcome to each conflict, and the explanation for each mystery.

In *Sweet Sweetback's Baadasssss Song*, after its protagonist appears to have escaped from his pursuers across the Mexican border, the film ends with zooming screen text which proclaims:

> Watch out – WATCH OUT – A Baadasssss Nigger Is Coming Back to Collect Some Dues.

This provides the narrative with only partial closure, because we do not actually see him escape, and because the screen text suggests that the story is far from over. It also reflects the film's revolutionary theme in suggesting that black rebellion will continue.

Narrative theories can throw light on the text, although some can be complicated to apply, eg Vladimir Propp's eight spheres of action and 31 functions. Claude Lévi-Strauss's binary oppositions can often reveal the underlying conflicts and values in a story's themes; Tzvetan Todorov's idea of equilibrium can be applied to show the dynamics of screen drama in a very straightforward way; and for A Level/National Diploma students, two of Roland Barthes' narrative codes – enigma and action – usually suffice.

See also **Worksheet 13**.

To access student worksheets and other online materials go to *Teaching Black Cinema* at **www.bfi.org.uk/tfms** and enter User name: **blackcine@bfi.org.uk** and Password: **te2007bl**.

Narrative theory can be applied practically as part of coursework preparation where students are learning how to write their own scripts: books by screenwriting gurus such as Syd Field, Robert McKee and Christopher Vogler, suitably filleted, can offer students an insight into story structure, to the benefit of their own work.

● Genre

The study of genre in black cinema can be equally revealing. We have already put forward the view that black cinema is itself too broad a category to constitute a genre, although blaxploitation is the most obvious candidate – see p.59. We can see generic conventions of all kinds being adopted by various films with black themes, such as the costume drama (*Amistad*), the thriller (*The Defiant Ones*), the crime drama (*In the Heat of the Night*), the musical (*Carmen Jones*, Otto Preminger, US, 1954) and the comedy (*Soul Plane*, Jessy Terrero, US, 2004). As a classroom exercise in pairs, students could draw up a longish list of recent movies that might be described as black cinema, and categorise them according to genre. This could then be compared with a more general list of mainstream Hollywood movies. Do some genres, such as crime and comedy, predominate in the 'black' list, and are some quite scarce, such as romance? How might we account for these differences?

The genre issue should also be turned around to examine how black characters are represented in mainstream Hollywood genres – not only in relation to tokenism, but in sports and science-fiction films, and in buddy films like *Silver Streak* (Arthur Hiller, US, 1976), *48 Hrs.* (Walter Hill, US, 1982) and *Lethal Weapon* (Richard Donner, US, 1987).

● Close textual readings

Close textual readings of brief film sequences are an essential way of helping students to focus on small but important details that they might not otherwise notice. Teachers can choose a brief (around ten minutes) sequence from a film and devise a set of four or five questions about it. The sequence is then played two or three times, and the students should provide textual evidence for their written answers. The questions may focus on any combination of micro or macro elements. Several suggested close textual readings are provided in Section 3.

Let us take as an example a scene near the beginning of *In the Heat of the Night*. Sidney Poitier plays detective Virgil Tibbs, who has been mistakenly arrested for murder in a small Mississippi town. Bill Gillespie, the police chief, played by Rod Steiger, does not yet know that Tibbs is also a policeman. See **Worksheet 5** (See p26).

Mise en scène and performance

Defined as whatever visual elements the director has decided to include in a scene, the *mise en scène* incorporates the set or location, props, lighting, costumes, hair and makeup, and the ways in which actors and physical objects move or are positioned within the frame. These elements are crucial to establishing mood and a sense of period and place.

The scene just referred to takes place at night in Gillespie's dingy office, which is poorly lit, with shadows often thrown across Gillespie's face. Gillespie wears a crumpled, short-sleeved shirt unbuttoned at the neck. This contrasts with Tibbs's crisp dark suit and tie. Character movement is also important: Gillespie chews gum, moves about restlessly behind his desk or lounges back in his chair with his feet up on the desk, his gaze wandering here and there. Tibbs, meanwhile, stands motionless throughout, his eyes fixed on Gillespie. When Tibbs eventually leaves the room, his movements are brisk and economical, compared with Gillespie's slovenly gait.

Cinematography

Here we are looking at the way the camera is used, defined by the shot size, angle, level, focus and movement. This scene is shot in a straightforward and conventional style. However, rather than beginning with an establishing shot, it starts with a close-up of Tibbs in the doorway, followed by a reverse angle close-up on Gillespie, who is stooped over next to an air-conditioning unit. There is minimal camera movement during their initial verbal exchanges, until Tibbs throws his police badge on to the desk. The significance of this is suggested by the camera tilting down and then up. From now on the seated Gillespie is shown from a high angle, while for the standing Tibbs, the camera moves to a lower level to show him from a low, more dominant angle. This may suggest that the balance of power has shifted during the scene.

Sound

We usually break sound down into its main components – dialogue, music and sound effects. There will also be barely audible ambient sound, or 'atmosphere'. Silence is a further aspect of the soundtrack that can be used to great effect. Here, the dialogue between Gillespie and Tibbs is punctuated by silences, as Gillespie tries to intimidate his prisoner. The tension of the scene is underlined by the lack of music, which has been present in earlier scenes. Sound effects are important here too: the squeaks, clanks and whirrs of the malfunctioning air-conditioning unit give the impression of an office where things do not work very effectively. A little later, a train whistle blows in the distance, backing up Tibbs' story that he is only in town to catch a particular train – which he has now missed.

Editing

Continuity editing is the style most commonly used in drama, to give the impression of action taking place in real time. This disguises the reality of filmmaking, in which it can take months to make a film whose plot may evolve over a few fictional hours. (Montage is a style more likely to be used in action sequences.) In this film, since we are considering a key scene in which the protagonists meet for the first time, the director's job is to ensure that the audience are not distracted from the key factors of character and plot by any intrusive editing. He therefore keeps the cutting smooth and simple. The length of the shots during the more tense verbal exchanges is short, but otherwise the tempo of the scene is quite evenly paced, with plenty of reaction shots included so that the audience can assess how the characters are relating to each other and the revelations of the plot.

Representation

● Auteurs

One of the many problematics of film studies is the existence or otherwise of the auteur – the author of the film. There is not space in a short guide like this to rehearse the full history of auteur criticism; however, for those who are new to it, several resources are recommended in the bibliography.

As a collaborative process, filmmaking demands creative and artistic contributions from a large number of people – not only the director but also studio executives, writers, producers, actors, production designer, director of photography, sound designer and editor. Every department head has a large staff, each of whom has something of their own to add to the look or sound of the film: even a relatively low-budget production such as Denzel Washington's directorial debut *Antwone Fisher* (US, 2002) credits 75 crew members in the art department alone. Most of a director's time on the set is taken up with making decisions at every level, from discussing with the star the interpretation of a scene, right down to choosing the colour of a minor character's tie.

The question students must answer is therefore how far can the completed film be credited to the director? This is in order to establish to what extent it can be considered the director's own self-expressive artistic statement or vision, in the same way as a poem by Carol Ann Duffy or an art installation by Tracey Emin. The difference between film and the other arts is the enormously high level of capital investment required to bring it into being. Film funding depends on the likelihood of a return on the financier's investment, which in turn depends on sales of tickets and DVDs. We must therefore take into account the commercial realities of the film industry when making judgements about artistic merit. The director is likely to have made compromises.

The most prominent auteur in modern American black cinema, and the most successful, is Spike Lee, who has explored themes of blackness and black history throughout his career. He has done this in accessible and entertaining ways, which make his films ideal as introductory study for students. Section 3 of this guide contains a case study of his career. See also **Worksheet 12** (p26).

There are other black directors with a distinctive personal style: Keenen Ivory Wayans has enjoyed major success in comedy as an actor, writer and producer, and as director of the blaxploitation spoof *I'm Gonna Git You Sucka*, *Low Down Dirty Shame* (US, 1994), the first two *Scary Movie* releases (US, 2000, 2001) and *White Chicks* (US, 2004). Members of his large family are also frequently involved. Charles Burnett is a highly regarded independent who has gained major critical success with *Killer of Sheep* (US, 1977) and *To Sleep with Anger* (US, 1990), although most of his recent work has been in television.

● **Black American directors**

Spike Lee's trailblazing led to a burst of black filmmaking in the early 1990s in the US, many of them 'hood' movies with more than a touch of the blaxploitation update to them. Most notably these included John Singleton's *Boyz N the Hood*, Matty Rich's *Straight out of Brooklyn*, Mario Van Peebles' *New Jack City*, Charles Lane's *True Identity* (featuring Lenny Henry), Bill Duke's *A Rage in Harlem*, and one lone female director, Julie Dash, with the art film *Daughters of the Dust* (all US, 1991). Other new black directors were Ernest Dickerson (*Juice*, 1992; *Blind Faith*, 1998), Albert and Allen Hughes (*Menace II Society*, 1993; *Dead Presidents*, 1995), Carl Franklin (*One False Move*, 1992; *Devil in a Blue Dress*, 1995), F. Gary Gray (*Friday*, 1995; *Set It Off*, 1996), George Tillman Jr (*Soul Food*, 1997) and Kasi Lemmons (*Eve's Bayou*, 1997). Another notable film was *Fresh* (1994) directed by Boaz Yakin.

John Singleton has gone on to make (or re-make) *Shaft* (2000) and *Four Brothers* (2005); Mario Van Peebles' work has included *Panther* (1995) and *Baadasssss!* (2003). Newer black directors include Antoine Fuqua (*Training Day*, 2001), Damon Dash and David Daniel (*Paper Soldiers*, 2002), Rick Famuyiwa (*The Wood*, 1999; *Brown Sugar*, 2002), Tim Story (*Barbershop*, 2002; *Fantastic Four,* 2005), Kevin Rodney Sullivan (*How Stella Got Her Groove Back*, 1998; *Barbershop 2: Back in Business*, 2004; and *Guess Who*, 2005) and Gina Prince-Bythewood (*Love and Basketball*, 2000).

Today black directors work both in TV and in the Hollywood mainstream – where no black director had ever worked until 1969 (Gordon Parks with *The Learning Tree*). Tim Story with *Fantastic Four* (2005) is but one recent example.

● Women in black American cinema

The representation of women in black American cinema, both behind and in front of the camera, has proved as controversial as the topic as a whole. We have already referred to the few stereotyped roles available to black women up to and including the 1970s. However, in a broader sense of the term, representation also refers to the presence of women in key production roles, particularly as directors. It could be said that black women directors face not one but two disadvantages merely by virtue of being black and female. Certainly there have been few directors matching that description since the 1980s.

Women directors

Julie Dash's *Daughters of the Dust* finally appeared in 1990 following the director's ten-year struggle to get it made. It is a poetic and highly visual film set in the early 20th century about a family of women preparing to leave their home on the Sea Islands off the South Carolina coast. They are from the Gullah community – descendants of West African-born slaves, with their own unique creole dialect and traditions. Another costume drama, *Eve's Bayou* is set in the early 1960s and tells its story through the eyes of a young girl. It was directed by former actress Kasi Lemmons and features Jurnee Smollett, Meagan Good and Samuel L Jackson as a well-to-do family which suffers from the philandering of its father, a doctor. Respected critic Roger Ebert considered this the best film of 1997, yet Lemmons has made only one film since.

Novelist and actress Maya Angelou directed *Down in the Delta* (US, 1998), another Southern-set drama, which features a poor family struggling to get by in rural Mississippi. Made by Wesley Snipes' production company, it also features him, along with Alfre Woodard and Al Freeman Jr. *Love and Basketball* is a romantic drama directed by Gina Prince-Bythewood and produced by Spike Lee. It stars Sanaa Lathan and Omar Epps as a couple of well-heeled black teenagers and focuses on the pressures put on their relationship by the demands of sporting excellence.

Civil Brand (US, 2002) is a drama directed by experienced TV director Neema Barnette. Starring N'Bushe Wright, LisaRaye and Mos Def, it tells the story of slave labour in a privatised women's prison. *My Baby's Daddy* (US, 2004), was directed by African-born Cheryl Dunye for Miramax, and is a comedy in the vein of *Three Men and a Baby* and *Look Who's Talking*. It features Eddie Griffin, Anthony Anderson and Michael Imperioli as three bachelors whose girlfriends all become pregnant at the same time.

Students may find it interesting to discuss why it might be important that women are given the chance to direct films, with creative control over representation and subject matter, since this question may be applied equally to anyone who is not white, male or American. This discussion might include the issue of whether women's experience might cause them to see the world differently from men, and the ways in which a woman director might relate to two traditionally male domains: the film crew and technology. This could then lead to consideration of the social and cultural factors which may affect black women in particular.

Women on screen

Many commentators have remarked on the shortage of black women in the top rank of Hollywood stars (albeit matched only by the shortage of white female stars). One or two movies have attempted to remedy this, notably Forest Whitaker's big screen debut as director, *Waiting to Exhale* (US, 1995). Another success was George Tillman Jr's comedy *Soul Food*, starring Vanessa L Williams, Vivica Fox and Nia Long in the story of three sisters and their marriages within an extended working black family, headed by a strong matriarch. Other actresses to come to the fore in recent years include Jada Pinkett Smith and Queen Latifah. However, even high-profile success is no guarantee of a future career: British actress Marianne Jean-Baptiste was nominated for an Oscar in 1996 (for Mike Leigh's *Secrets and Lies*) but found parts very hard to come by afterwards.

Angela Bassett is the common factor in many significant films involving black actresses since the 1980s. She was nominated for an Oscar in her role as Tina Turner in *What's Love Got to Do with It* (Brian Gibson, US, 1993), having been cast for a second time with Laurence Fishburne as her husband (they were previously paired as the parents in *Boyz N the Hood*). In *Waiting to Exhale*, she was part of an ensemble including Whitney Houston, Loretta Devine and Lela Rochon as four middle-class friends with men problems. Despite lukewarm notices from largely male reviewers, the film went on to be a major hit with black American women. (See **Worksheet 18**.) In *How Stella Got Her Groove Back*, Bassett plays a middle-aged bond trader who takes a holiday in Jamaica with her friend (played by Whoopi Goldberg) and embarks on an affair with a young black man half her age (Taye Diggs).[9]

To access student worksheets and other online materials go to *Teaching Black Cinema* at **www.bfi.org.uk/tfms** and enter User name: **blackcine@bfi.org.uk** and Password: **te2007bl**.

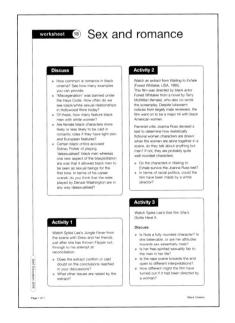

[9] *How Stella Got Her Groove Back*, *Soul Food* and *Waiting to Exhale* are available on DVD as a triple pack.

British stars Thandie Newton and Sophie Okonedo (Oscar-nominated for *Hotel Rwanda*, Terry George, US/UK/Italy/South Africa, 2004) have made a significant impact in Hollywood in recent years, but Halle Berry is the only black woman to be ranked in the top ten highest-paid actresses in Hollywood, following her Oscar success with *Monster's Ball* (Marc Forster, US) in 2002. She has maintained a high profile in both the *X-Men* films (2000 and 2003) and the Bond thriller *Die Another Day* (Lee Tamahori, UK/US, 2002). However, at the age of 40 she will soon confront the problem all Hollywood actresses eventually face – the shortage of parts for older women.

Brief case studies of Dorothy Dandridge and Sidney Poitier are provided in Section 3.

Love and sex

Hollywood's squeamishness over mixed-race romance has persisted, as American audiences continue to struggle with the concept of interracial love and sex. What examples can students come up with, and how many of these feature black women with white men rather than vice versa? If a disparity is found, why might this be?

A further issue which should be debated is whether the black male hero has once again become desexualised in modern Hollywood, after a brief period in the 1970s when he was allowed both white and black sexual partners.

Bogle points out that in *The Pelican Brief* (Alan J Pakula, US, 1993), Denzel Washington and Julia Roberts are not permitted to become lovers, as their characters do in the original book. He suggests that times have not changed much since 1967's *Guess Who's Coming to Dinner*, when the romance between Sidney Poitier and Katharine Houghton is limited to a single kiss right at the start, seen in a cab driver's rearview mirror. In both *Training Day* and *Hitch*, it is notable that Denzel Washington and Will Smith are given Hispanic lovers, which may appear to some like Hollywood's idea of compromise.

Monster's Ball and *She Hate Me* (Spike Lee, US, 2004) both raise questions about how male directors represent black women sexually. In her previous film *Swordfish* (Dominic Sena, US, 2001), Halle Berry reveals her breasts, for reasons which remain narratively obscure; in *Monster's Ball* she reveals all in a lengthy sex scene – this time justified by the plot – with white actor Billy Bob Thornton. In *Die Another Day*, she goes to bed with white actor Pierce Brosnan – who is, after all, James Bond.

In the Spike Lee sex comedy *She Hate Me*, wealthy lesbians pay $10,000 a time to be impregnated by sacked business executive Anthony Mackie. His clients include his ex-girlfriend (played by Kerry Washington), her girlfriend and the daughter of a Mafia crime boss. Despite the fact that the film was intended as a comedy, and despite hiring a 'lesbian sexuality expert' in an attempt to achieve some degree of authenticity, the director was criticised by lesbian groups and critics alike.

Thandie Newton is a light-skinned, European-featured actress of mixed race. In *Crash* (Paul Haggis, US/Germany, 2004), she and her black husband are pulled over by racist cop Matt Dillon, who proceeds to grope her at length while the husband looks on, helpless to intervene. Would audiences interpret this deeply uncomfortable scene differently if she were darker and more African-featured? The same question could be asked regarding the consensual sex scenes involving Halle Berry and white actors. See **Worksheet 10**.

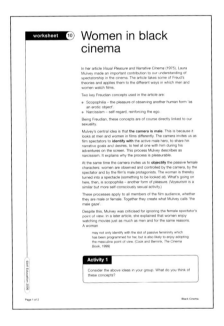

To access student worksheets and other online materials go to *Teaching Black Cinema* at **www.bfi.org.uk/tfms** and enter User name: **blackcine@bfi.org.uk** and Password: **te2007bl**.

One consideration for students therefore is whether they think films like these exploit women by appealing to male fantasies, and whether they promote racial and/or sexual stereotypes.

Finally, there may be a disparity between black leading men and women in 'allowable' skin colour: for example, Wesley Snipes, Denzel Washington and Samuel L Jackson are all dark-skinned, with no apparent detriment to their star status; however, it does seem to make a difference with the women, the more successful of whom have been lighter-skinned and European-featured (Whitney Houston, Halle Berry, Thandie Newton), while darker actresses like Angela Bassett and Whoopi Goldberg appear to have been under appreciated.

● The influence of hip-hop

While 'race films' died out in the 1930s, 'race records' were followed by a burgeoning crossover appeal of black music to white audiences that has continued ever since. As the 20th century progressed, music – along with sport – became the arena in which black people could aspire to fame and fortune on an equal footing with whites.

Beginning with jazz, and continuing with rock and roll, soul and funk, this process has culminated today in hip-hop becoming *the* mainstream pop music of the world. Visual images of this black culture are therefore highly significant to all of today's young people, contributing on a global level not merely to clothing but to language and lifestyle. One useful entry point for the whole discussion of black cinema would therefore be contemporary black music videos, which for years have been influenced by blaxploitation films. See **Worksheet 16**.

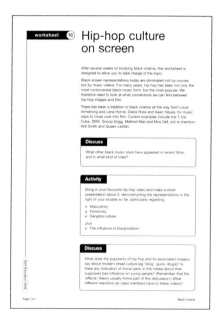

To access student worksheets and other online materials go to *Teaching Black Cinema* at **www.bfi.org.uk/tfms** and enter User name: **blackcine@bfi.org.uk** and Password: **te2007bl**.

Spike Lee has criticised the 'bling' lifestyle and 'gangsta' attitudes of performers like 50 Cent, who boast about the number of times they have been shot:

> I don't think they are elevating black culture. When your CD is entitled Get Rich or Die Trying, that is not about elevation. (Aftab, 2005)

In *Bullet Boy*, Rio, a young schoolboy, is accidentally shot by his friend Curtis. Later, in hospital, far from being angry or upset, he can't wait to get back to school where he knows it will greatly impress the other children.

One recent trend in hip-hop has been its link with the pornography industry. Stars such as Snoop Dogg (in 'Doggystyle' and 'Diary of a Pimp'), 50 Cent and Lil Jon have presented videos featuring hardcore pornography with a hip-hop soundtrack. DJ Yella, a former member of the rap group NWA, now makes his living from producing pornographic films. However, there is nothing new in black men depicting themselves as pimps and the women around them as whores. In the autobiographical novels of Iceberg Slim and in such blaxploitation films as *The Mack* (Michael Campus, US, 1973), the pimp is seen as a black urban hero, a successful trickster who lives on his wits and gains respect on the street for his ability to control women.

The black feminist writer bell hooks refuses to pin the blame on young black men for embracing sexism and misogyny. She argues that rap music did not emerge from some black cultural vacuum, but that young blacks are influenced by the same cultural norms as society as a whole, particularly

> privileged white culture [which] … has historically romanticized primitivism and eroticized male violence. Contemporary films … exploit the cultural demand for depictions of hardcore blacks who are willing to kill for sport.[10]

● Stars

A notable change since the early 1990s' watershed has been the permission granted to black stars to headline in Hollywood films with no black theme to them. In other words, as mentioned in Section 1, parts for black actors may now be based on ability rather than race.

Students can carry out a standard commutation test to assess the relevance, if any, of a star's race to their part in a film. This merely requires them to consider how different the film would be with a white actor playing the role. For example, Will Smith in *Independence Day* (Roland Emmerich, US, 1996), *Enemy of the State* or *Hitch*.

Despite the apparent wealth of black talent on the big screen today, some problems remain. It has been pointed out that skin tone and physiognomy have an influence on casting decisions. Even in the 'race' films of Oscar Micheaux, the hero would generally be lighter-skinned than the other black characters. Students may discuss whether a 'black' actor with European-type features, such as Halle Berry (whose white mother is English-born), is more likely to find favour in a romantic role than one with a more African look, such as Whoopi Goldberg.

---

[10] From her essay 'Sexism and Mysogyny: Who Takes the Rap?' (1994).

Older stars whose careers would make interesting and appropriate research subjects include Paul Robeson, Stepin Fetchit, Hatty McDaniel, Lena Horne, Dorothy Dandridge and Sidney Poitier. These studies could throw light on the limitations on allowable roles for black characters under the Hollywood studio system. See **Worksheets 4** (p28) and **5** (p26).

Stepin Fetchit appeared in over 50 films during the 1920s and 30s. He was usually cast as a stereotypically lazy, bumbling farmhand, stable boy or slave – the dim-witted comic relief with bulging eyes and slow speech. But few of his films have been released on DVD, and that includes some of his major roles for Fox such as in *Hearts in Dixie* (Paul Sloane, US, 1929) and *Steamboat round the Bend* (John Ford, US, 1935).[11] It is important for students to know about his career, however, particularly when they learn that he was the first black actor to become a millionaire, and wore $1,000 cashmere suits. At one time he owned 12 cars including a pink Rolls-Royce with his name in neon lights along the side, and employed a staff of 16 Chinese servants. His comic timing was apparently admired by Charlie Chaplin and Buster Keaton, but he was vilified in later life for the demeaning roles he played.

From the perspective of the early 21st century, Paul Robeson appears like a man born before his time. Between 1925 and 1942 he appeared in 11 films, all but four of them British, having moved from the USA to England in the late 1920s. At the height of his popularity in the 1930s, Robeson became a major box-office attraction in British films such as *Song of Freedom* and *The Proud Valley* (Pen Tennyson, UK, 1940). He returned briefly to the USA to film *The Emperor Jones* (Dudley Murphy, US, 1933) and the 1936 version of *Show Boat* (James Whale, US). He was eventually blacklisted by Hollywood for his political beliefs.

The influence of hip-hop and music stars is once again worth stressing. There has been a tradition in black cinema all the way from Louis Armstrong and Lena Horne, Diana Ross and Isaac Hayes, for music stars to cross over into film. Others include Ice-T, Ice Cube, DMX, Snoop Dogg, Method Man and Mos Def, not to mention Will Smith and Queen Latifah. Of course, students will be able to furnish additional and perhaps more recent examples.

● Stereotyping

Donald Bogle, in his book *Toms, Coons, Mulattoes, Mammies and Bucks: An Interpretive History of Blacks in American Films* (2003), put forward the thesis that there were, and had only ever been, five stereotypical roles available to

---

[11] Determined fans can find him playing (uncredited) Shirley Temple's servant in the 1936 20th Century-Fox film *Dimples* (William A Seiter, US), which is available on DVD.

black actors in Hollywood films. (See **Worksheet 1**, p13.) These stereotypes, in turn, are derived from the stock characters of 19th-century blackface minstrel shows.

- A Tom, according to Bogle, is an Uncle Tom, based on the eponymous 'hero' of Harriet Beecher Stowe's famous anti-slavery novel *Uncle Tom's Cabin*, first published in 1852. The Tom is any noble, long-suffering slave-mentality character, who passively allows whites to walk all over him. Sidney Poitier was accused of playing Tom-style characters in films such as *The Defiant Ones* and *Guess Who's Coming to Dinner*.

- The Coon stereotype is a pop-eyed, shuffling, singing, dancing clown, ignorant and fearful, the butt of white people's jokes and, like the Tom, quite harmless. Stepin Fetchit is perhaps the archetypal Coon. Spike Lee parodies this type of character in his satire *Bamboozled* (US, 2000).

- The Mulatto is a mixed-race character to whom the epithet 'tragic' is often attached. The reason for this is that since blackness was regarded as a taint, a single drop of black blood 'condemned' a person to blackness, even if they were 75% white. 'Passing' as white was something a Mulatto in films would try to do, leading invariably to their 'unmasking' and subsequent confrontation with white characters who had thought he or she was 'one of them'. In Elia Kazan's *Pinky* (US, 1949), Jeanne Crain (a white actress) plays a light-skinned trainee nurse who fails to tell her white doctor boyfriend about her black heritage.

- The Mammie was just about the only role available to most black actresses up until the 1940s, and sometimes beyond. The best-known example of this stereotype is Hattie McDaniel's Mammy, Scarlett O'Hara's overweight, long-suffering, irascible housekeeper in *Gone with the Wind* (Victor Fleming, US, 1939). (McDaniel went on to play a very similar character in the early TV series *Beulah* in 1950 shortly before she died.) Another example is the unnamed and unseen (above the waist) black housemaid, who is the scourge of Tom the cat in the MGM animated series *Tom and Jerry*.

- The Buck is the only stereotype who, Bogle claims, poses any threat to whites. He is the physically powerful, sexually potent, rebellious black character who is able and willing to exact revenge on whites. Not only will he confront white men, but ravish white women, who may indeed be attracted to him. The out-of-control heroes of blaxploitation fit this particular cinematic mould, with such characters as Sweetback in *Sweet Sweetback's Baadasssss Song*, John Shaft, and Priest in *Superfly*.

As well as trying to identify examples of Bogle's stereotypes, students will naturally want to discuss and test the validity of his theories – not just in films from the 1960s and before, but in current ones. The Buck came strongly to the fore in the blaxploitation films of the 1970s, and a version of him may well be evident in any modern action thriller starring Wesley Snipes, but perhaps with a difference: the blaxploitation buck was allowed to be sexual, often having white girlfriends. Today this is rare indeed. Has the Mammie disappeared? Watch Wanda Sykes as the servant Ruby in *Monster-in Law* (Robert Luketic, US, 2005). And do students detect any echoes of the Coon in some of Eddie Murphy's less successful roles?

Donald Bogle has insisted that some black stereotyping remains in modern cinema. In Robert Redford's much-criticised film *The Legend of Bagger Vance* (US, 2000), Will Smith plays a golf caddie to Matt Damon in the kind of servant role that seemed to many like a relic of the 1930s.

Bogle also points out what he considers to be the retro depiction of the character John Coffey in *The Green Mile* (Frank Darabont, US, 1999). Wrongly accused of a double child rape and murder, Coffey – a black 'gentle giant' type – is a humble, self-sacrificing character with supernatural healing powers whom some saw as a racial caricature, a 'Tom'. Students may be able to suggest further examples of the stereotypical black mystic who possesses deep spiritual/tribal knowledge, eg Scatman Crothers in *The Shining* (Stanley Kubrick, US, 1980), Whoopi Goldberg in *Ghost* (Jerry Zucker, US, 1990) and Gloria Foster as the Oracle in *The Matrix*.

Things are less clear cut in the black–white buddy film: the formula established by Richard Pryor and Gene Wilder in their comedies *Stir Crazy* (Sidney Poitier, US, 1980) and *Silver Streak* (1976) was adapted in *48 Hrs.* (1982) by Eddie Murphy and Nick Nolte, with Murphy as the 'crazy' half of the duo. However, in the *Lethal Weapon* series (1987–98), it is Mel Gibson who steals the limelight with his crazed antics, while Danny Glover is the sensible (and less interesting) one (see **Worksheet 1**, p13). In *Se7en*, it is possible to see the Morgan Freeman character as little more than a foil for the real star Brad Pitt, who is allowed to take centre stage and hog the action scenes while Freeman merely provides the gravitas. A counter argument is that these roles are at least non-stereotypical, in terms of Bogle's system.

Black filmmakers can also be accused of perpetuating stereotypes: for example, controversy raged over Jessy Terrero's 2004 comedy *Soul Plane*. See **Worksheet 17**. It could be argued that the stoned black pilot, the built-in dancefloor in the hold of the plane and the pimp style décor are jokes aimed at the stereotypes rather than at black people themselves. But the imdb message board was split on the issue, some black audience members finding the film deeply offensive, others insisting it was only a comedy. One commented:

Do you ever watch a movie just to watch? I mean, really – not every movie is out there to cast off stereotypes or to open people's eyes to what's really out there. Some movies are just there to make fun of those stereotypes.

To access student worksheets and other online materials go to *Teaching Black Cinema* at **www.bfi.org.uk/tfms** and enter User name: **blackcine@bfi.org.uk** and Password: **te2007bl**.

Spectatorship, particularly black spectatorship, is therefore an important issue, and it is important not to assume that all black audiences are 'seeing' a film in the same way as white audiences, or as each other as individuals.

It may not be immediately apparent to students, particularly with films they like, that representations are often more complex and many-faceted than they appear. Is *Soul Plane*'s target audience sophisticated enough to distinguish between irony and cliché? Is it acknowledging that there is some truth in the stereotypes? Are films like *Soul Plane* the only black films that can attract funding? Or are they the only black films that attract audiences?

Encouraging students to apply their knowledge of black cinema to modern films should be done delicately: pointing out a possible flaw in a film does not necessarily condemn the whole thing to failure, and in any case it is important to open these matters to classroom debate rather than lay down the law on what is, after all, a matter of personal interpretation.

3

Case studies

Introduction

The previous two sections have suggested several possible areas of study. This one highlights six of these, with more detailed information and further suggestions about how they may be taught, making connections with the worksheets. The worksheets also include close textual readings from certain key films: *The Birth of a Nation*, *Gone with the Wind*, *In the Heat of the Night, Sweet Sweetback's Baadasssss Song, Do the Right Thing, The Hurricane* and *Bullet Boy*.

1. Slavery is the common historical background to most English-speaking black cultures outside Africa (although today African immigration to the West is clearly influencing and changing them). The representation of black people in early Hollywood cinema tells us much about how white society viewed slavery and its aftermath. *The Birth of a Nation* and *Gone with the Wind* were phenomenal commercial successes in their day.

2. Hollywood was closed to black filmmakers before the 1970s and black actors found it difficult to shake off the stereotypical, often demeaning, roles allotted to them. This began to change in the 1950s, but controversy and debate continued, and while Sidney Poitier made historic breakthroughs, Dorothy Dandridge's career never achieved its potential.

3. The influence of blaxploitation is still being felt. In some cases the films were produced by black filmmakers, but from the audience's point of view it marked the first time black actors could take on assertive, culturally 'black' roles in which their characters came out on top. *Sweet Sweetback's Baadasssss Song* is generally acknowledged as the first of these.

4. Spike Lee is a cultural icon who has become a spokesman for black America, with an unequalled 20-year career as a filmmaker and actor. His films have tackled numerous social issues from a black perspective, and with *Do the Right Thing* he created a storm of controversy – the first of many.

5. As well as being one of the highest-paid stars in Hollywood, of any race, Denzel Washington achieved the distinction of winning the Academy Award for Best Actor for his role in *Training Day*, only the second black man to do so. He has played roles in which his race is an issue, and others in which it is not. In *The Hurricane*, he plays the kind of noble black character which made him famous.

6. Recent years have seen signs of a revival in filmmaking from a black British perspective. Two films released in 2004 – *A Way of Life* and *Bullet Boy* – built on the British realist tradition to tell stories about family life, in which combinations of race, poverty and working-class culture prove highly destructive.

Case study 1: Images of slavery

● Context and historical background

Slavery was a trade in human beings lasting nearly 400 years and resulting in the kidnapping and transportation across the Atlantic Ocean of an estimated 12 million people, a large proportion of whom died on the way. The trade resulted in the total destruction of the Africans' communities, family lives and social structure, a process that continued on the plantations of the New World. It is not surprising that the cultural reverberations of slavery continue to be felt today.

The American Civil War ended in 1865 with victory for the anti-slavery union forces of the North. The slaves were legally freed a few months later, and the following 12 years were known as the Reconstruction, during which many Civil Rights laws were passed including those legalising interracial marriage and funding integrated public education. Former slaves were given senior posts in the government, often as state senators, legislators, judges, mayors, sheriffs or deputy governors.

In retaliation, white Southerners, often led by former Confederate officers, formed vigilante organisations like the Ku Klux Klan. At the same time, the former slave-owning states of the South began to challenge the newly passed Reconstruction legislation in the Supreme Court. As a result, over the years which followed, blacks gradually resumed their previous low status: in 1883 it was established that discrimination against them was only illegal if it was 'public' rather than 'private'; in 1896 segregation became legal once again, as long as 'separate but equal' facilities were provided for whites and blacks. Petty 'Jim Crow' laws, concerning such matters as the use of drinking fountains and public lavatories, continued to be passed up until 1915, in addition to a whole unwritten code of subservient behaviour expected of black people in their dealings with whites.[12]

It was against this background, in 1891, that Thomas Edison's laboratory staff built the first kinetograph (a motion picture camera) and kinetoscope (a peep-hole motion picture viewer). The very earliest images captured on film in America included such titles as *The Pickaninnies* (anon, US, 1894) and *Dancing Darkey Boy* (anon, US, 1897).[13] Once more legally relegated to second-class citizens, 'negroes' were seen as 'other', people who were comically different from the norm. In these early films, they were frequently depicted as dancers, chicken thieves and eaters of watermelon.

● *The Birth of a Nation*

The most successful silent film ever made, D W Griffith's *The Birth of a Nation* was not overtaken at the box office until 1937.[14] (See **Worksheet 3**, p14.) It was a true epic, running for over three hours and with a sweeping historical theme covering the period from before the Civil War to its aftermath, alongside a more intimate story of two families. In making the film, Griffith, the son of a Confederate colonel and war veteran, had adapted a play called *The Clansman*, written by North Carolina Baptist minister and white supremacist the Rev. Thomas Dixon.

As well as pleasing white audiences of the day with its heroic depictions of the Ku Klux Klan, and correspondingly demeaning portrayals of its black characters, it also popularised a host of new filmic techniques and hence served afterwards as the technical rule book for film directors. These techniques included extensive camera movement – panning and tracking shots; the use of full-screen close-ups to allow more subtle and naturalistic acting; and complex cross-cutting between scenes to generate excitement and suspense.

Despite its success, the film's portrayal of blacks provoked widespread anger. Protests were led by the recently formed NAACP (National Association for the Advancement of Colored Peoples) and eight states banned it altogether. Nonetheless, *The Birth of a Nation* was re-released every year up until the mid-1920s, and was credited with reviving the previously dormant Ku Klux Klan, who used it as a recruiting tool and felt sufficiently emboldened by their improved fortunes to mount huge parades through major cities.

---

[12] For example, a black man could not offer to shake a white man's hand, or even look at a white woman. When speaking to a white person, a black had to refer to him or her as 'Sir, 'Mister,' or 'Ma'am', while whites called blacks by their first names, or simply 'boy'. If blacks and whites were in the same car, truck, or bus, blacks rode in the back. Blacks who failed to observe these rules ran the risk of being lynched.

[13] These and others can be viewed at http://www.indiana.edu/~bfca/clips.html.

[14] By Walt Disney's *Snow White and the Seven Dwarfs*.

The Birth of a Nation caused controversy over its simplistic representation of whites as heroes and blacks as 'crazed Negroes' who had to be stopped from causing anarchy, from lusting after white women and – ultimately – from exercising their newly won right to vote.

In the absence of sound, intertitles make plain how the audience were intended to interpret the film, although it veers in style between drama and documentary. The Camerons' plantation, where their slaves work contentedly in the cotton fields, is described as a place 'where life runs in a quaintly way that is to be no more'.

The term 'an historical facsimile' is used several times: for example, to indicate the re-staging (from photographs) of the formal signing of the Confederate surrender. This concern for accuracy did not extend to the use of black actors in any of the major black roles, which are played by very obviously white actors in blackface. Chief among these is the character of Silas Lynch (note the choice of surname), an ambitious mulatto who comes to power in North Carolina and tries to enact a forced marriage with a white woman – Elsie Stoneman, played by Lillian Gish. Two loyal house slaves who come to the rescue of the elderly Dr Cameron are also played by blacked-up whites.

In another noteworthy scene set in the North Carolina state legislature, blacks dominate the proceedings, and are shown eating, drinking liquor, taking off their boots and putting their bare feet up on the table. At the end of the scene there are big celebrations when they pass a bill allowing mixed marriages. These images were derived not from photographs, however, but from political cartoons.

Teachers may find it expedient to select extracts from this film, based on DVD chapters, rather than attempt a full screening. And although *The Birth of a Nation* came before *Gone with the Wind*, the context may be more readily appreciated if extracts from the latter are played first, with its benefits of sound and colour. However, the final scenes of *The Birth of a Nation* certainly deserve viewing at some length, with their fast editing, cross-cutting, big crowd scenes and stirring action.

● *Gone with the Wind*

Based on the number of people who paid to see it at the cinema, *Gone with the Wind* is generally reckoned to be the most popular film of all time, in both the US and the UK. (See **Worksheet 2**, p13.) The representations it contains are therefore very pertinent, since for many audiences the film was the most information they had received about slavery and the Old South since *The Birth of a Nation*. Certainly there are numerous similarities between the two films. Both are epics, hailed on release as the longest film ever made (*Gone with the*

Wind runs for nearly four hours), both are set in the South, cover the same historical period (the 1850s and 60s), and are supportive of slavery and the Southern way of life.

The first people we see in *Gone with the Wind* are black slaves toiling in the cotton fields. There are several explicit messages, both in the dialogue and in the screen text, that slaves were inferior beings whose lives were rightly at the disposal of their white owners. As Scarlett's father puts it:

> You must be firm with inferiors but you must be gentle with them, especially darkies.

The film's opening screen text describes this as a 'pretty world', a Golden Age in which

> gallantry took its last bow. Here was the last ever to be seen of Knights and their Ladies Fair …

By contrast, as the Union forces advance on the Confederate city of Atlanta, they are described as 'the oncoming Juggernaut' and 'the great Invader'. The Southerners, meanwhile, are 'Cavaliers'. As in *The Birth of a Nation*, the self-consciously quaint and courtly language speaks of a distant, prelapsarian world, when life was perfect and everyone knew their place.

Gone with the Wind is an important text for the study of black cinema because it features prominent roles for two black actresses, both portraying 'house slaves' – Hattie McDaniel as the grouchy but staunchly dependable Mammy and Butterfly McQueen as the half-witted hysteric Prissy. Not only did McDaniel win an Oscar as Best Supporting Actress in this film, but she was the first black American ever to be nominated for an Oscar.

As with *The Birth of a Nation*, it is possible that modern students will find these black representations laughable, or perhaps deeply offensive, but they should be encouraged to view the film in its proper historical context. Initially the characters do indeed appear as crass stereotypes – in Donald Bogle's scheme, Mammy as the archetypal Mammy, Prissy as a sort of female Coon, and the older male servant Pork as the Tom.

Yet even these characterisations indicate some degree of progress compared to previous roles available to black actors. McDaniel in particular is far from being the meek servant who simply follows the orders of her white masters. Her loyalty is without question, but on her first appearance in the film she is yelling angrily at the young Scarlett O'Hara from a window. She frequently complains about 'po' white trash'. While unswervingly devoted to Scarlett's welfare, she continues throughout the first part of the film to deplore her character and behaviour.

The black representations may be regarded as affectionate, albeit patronising, compared with the vicious portrayals in *The Birth of a Nation*. In a reversal of the 'Gus' sequence in *The Birth of a Nation*, Scarlett is rescued from two white attackers by Big Sam – a slave whom we meet briefly early in the film.

However, despite the chaos and destruction of the Civil War, we can read the film's message as one of continuity: even after the war, when all slaves have been freed, Mammy is still proud to serve. And when Scarlett's daughter is born, Mammy announces proudly:

> Dis sho' is a happy day to me. I done diapered three generations of this family's girls.

Meanwhile, however, the characters of Prissy, Pork and Big Sam have quietly disappeared from the story.

Students should avoid superficial 'good–bad' judgments and try to detect some of the more subtle undercurrents running through the film. For example, in analysing certain sequences, it is worth examining how the 'official' line is occasionally undermined. Despite having apparently lived through a Golden Age, none of the three main black servants appears particularly happy. Mammy is in a constant fret, anger bubbling just beneath the surface; Prissy is always frightened and unable to cope with stress; Pork is stooped and fearful, with the look of a man who has been beaten once too often. Implicit questions are raised all through the film about Scarlett's lack of moral scruples – especially towards the end when she takes over a sawmill and decides to staff it with cheap convict labour rather than 'free darkies'.

Case study 2: The struggle for equality

● Context and historical background

The 1950s was a key decade for black screen representation, seeing the emergence of two important stars whose careers students may investigate in order to assess evidence of social change, as well as the restrictions which black actors continued to face. In addition to analysing texts and considering the representations to be found in them, there are opportunities to address such key concepts as audience, industry, narrative and genre. Students may explore what subject matter and casting was deemed acceptable for audiences of the day and question how far, if at all, public attitudes appeared to have changed since the first half of the century. (See **Worksheet 5**.) How did Hollywood gauge the public mood, and were producers and studios in tune with it? Which genres were available to black performers, and which were closed to them? And finally, how do the narratives treat the black characters? For example, are their stories rooted in a personal history, or do the characters simply appear and disappear? In these ways we can begin to decode the messages and reveal the values of each film as a whole.

• Dorothy Dandridge

With only three of her films currently available on DVD, it seems strange to reflect that Dorothy Dandridge was a major screen star of the 1950s.[15] She was the first black female sex symbol, the first black performer of either sex to earn an Oscar nomination for a leading role (the musical *Carmen Jones*, Otto Preminger, US, 1954), and the first black woman ever to be embraced by a white actor on screen (*Island in the Sun*, Robert Rossen, US, 1957).[16] After starring in *Carmen Jones*, she found it difficult to obtain other roles. Her career was blighted, in part, by her refusal to be typecast. Her mixed-race 'mulatto' looks ensured she was always offered the part of a tragic, doomed character. Her ethnicity made her impossible to categorise in an era when an actor's race mattered more than their talent. As well as *Carmen Jones* and *Island in the Sun*, today she is remembered chiefly for her role in *Porgy and Bess* (Otto Preminger, US, 1959). She died of an overdose in 1964, aged 41.

As a star study, Dorothy Dandridge provides a prime example of an actress for whom the contemporary representations of blackness and womanhood became serious handicaps. The sexual and racial politics of the 1950s combined to restrict her to playing maids, sex sirens or whores. Students may wish to contrast her career not only with those of modern black female stars such as Halle Berry, who portrayed her in a 1999 TV biography, but with that of Sidney Poitier, who came to prominence at around the same time as Dorothy Dandridge.

• Sidney Poitier

The recognition paid to Sidney Poitier by today's black stars takes into account the restrictions he was under in the 1950s because of his race. And yet he became the first black actor able to command roles equal to whites, although these were limited in scope. Donald Bogle describes the Poitier screen persona as that of

> the model integrationist hero. In all his films he was educated and intelligent. He spoke proper English, dressed conservatively, and had the best of table manners. For the mass white audience, Sidney Poitier was a black man who had met their standards. His characters were tame; never did they act impulsively, nor were they threats to the system. They were amenable and pliant. And finally they were non-funky, almost sexless and sterile. In short, they were the perfect dream for white liberals anxious to have a colored man in for lunch or dinner.[17]

[15] *Carmen Jones*, *Porgy and Bess* and *Island in the Sun* are available on DVD.
[16] Audiences had to wait until 1967 for the first interracial kiss on the big screen, in *Guess Who's Coming to Dinner*. It happened on TV for the first time a year later, when William Shatner kissed Nichelle Nichols in an episode of *Star Trek*.
[17] Bogle (2003)

Bogle's reference is to *Guess Who's Coming to Dinner*, in which Poitier played just such a character – in this case a prominent physician and potential Nobel Prize winner who wishes to marry the daughter of a wealthy white liberal San Francisco family. It was a major commercial success. Students may wish to debate whether the quotation fully explains Sidney Poitier's success at a time when no other black actor was deemed acceptable as a film star.

Other significant films include: *The Defiant Ones* (1958), *Lilies of the Field* (1963), *To Sir with Love* (James Clavell, UK, 1967), *In the Heat of the Night* (1967) and *For the Love of Ivy* (Daniel Mann, US, 1968). He has also directed nine films, including the hugely successful Richard Pryor/Gene Wilder comedy *Stir Crazy* (1980).

As referred to throughout this guide, and as addressed by Bogle in the extract reproduced above, stereotyping has always been an issue for black actors. However, rather than dismiss black screen performances up to and including the 1960s because of it, students should be asked to consider the limitations of what was possible in the Jim Crow era. It would be more fruitful to observe what actors were able to achieve in the stereotypical roles they were given, as Hattie McDaniel did in *Gone with the Wind*. Students considering Poitier's acting career may also wish to make comparisons with that of Denzel Washington, seen by many as his natural heir.

Case study 3: Blaxploitation

● Context and historical background

If Sidney Poitier represented the white integrationist dream, the big screen anti-heroes of the blaxploitation era were its polar opposite. By the late 1960s, following the assassinations of John F Kennedy, Malcolm X and Martin Luther King, there was the feeling among many black Americans that the Mahatma Gandhi principle of achieving social reform through non-violent protest was getting them nowhere.

The resultant rise of black militancy saw a shift away from the politics of integration and towards Malcolm's policy of separatism. The Black Power movement, of which the Black Panthers became the best-known example, was now on the rise. (See **Worksheet 8**, p30.) At the same time a more positive social attitude was developing in the black community about its own culture. 'Natural' or 'Afro' hairstyles became popular, as did flamboyant African-style dashikis and fashion accessories. 'Black is beautiful' and 'Say it loud, I'm black and I'm proud' were two prominent slogans, while black self-expression in the arts was fostered by the Black Arts movement.

This new-found assertiveness and self-confidence was reflected in a new wave of black films in the early 1970s. The quiet moral rectitude of Poitier's characters was jettisoned and in its place came crime bosses, studs, pimps, ass-kicking detectives, drug dealers and political militants. As one critic put it, with blaxploitation

> you did not have to guess who was coming to dinner, these characters would kick the door in and announce themselves in no uncertain terms.

For the most part the films were lowbrow, low-budget action films produced as pure entertainment rather than as political statements. This fact has divided black critics and academics over the merits of blaxploitation, some seeing a strong connection between it and real-life criminality in the black community, attacking the films for irresponsibility, a mere acting-out of perverse fantasies. In the view of others, it was 'the true dawn of black filmmaking'.

A typical scenario is a three-sided contest between black protagonists, white police and the Mafia. In *Shaft* (1971), the protagonist is a private investigator hired by a black Harlem gangster to find his daughter, who it transpires has been kidnapped by the Mafia. Shaft accomplishes his task with the aid of a group of black militants. The police play a fairly peripheral role in the story and seem to be included largely so that Shaft can insult them.

Blaxploitation's uninhibited displays of violence, sex, drug-peddling and contempt for white people and the law, were something new in film at the time. However, later 'hood' movies such as *Menace II Society* and *New Jack City* were set in similar inner-city milieux and have focused on black crime, gang culture, violence and ghetto poverty. Modern commercial hip-hop culture often goes further in appearing to celebrate a nihilistic belief in pure individualism, fuelled by a combination of machismo and consumerism, and resulting in the phenomenon of ghetto chic, which originally surfaced in blaxploitation. These issues provide an opportunity for students to debate what possible social roles films play, and might be expected to play, in our culture.

Screening selections from available blaxploitation films should also provoke discussion about the nature of genre, along the lines of 'to what extent can blaxploitation be termed a genre?' This could be done by focusing on a particular star like Pam Grier, in films such as *Black Mama White Mama* (Eddie Romero, US/Philippines) – a distaff remake of *The Defiant Ones* from 1972, *Hit Man* (George Armitage, US, 1972), *Coffy* (Jack Hill, US, 1973), *Foxy Brown* (1974), *Bucktown* (Arthur Marks, US), *Sheba Baby* (William Girdler, US) and *Friday Foster* (Arthur Marks, US) (all 1975).

In *Coffy*, Grier plays a nurse surrounded by the victims and pushers of hard drugs, the former including her brother and 11-year-old sister. *Coffy* embarks on a campaign of merciless and bloodthirsty vengeance against the dealers and their accomplices. And in *Superfly*, the protagonist is himself a drug dealer who finds himself pitted against a white crime syndicate, whose head turns out to be the deputy commissioner of police. In this film, it is the black militants who are relatively peripheral.

We see repeated patterns in the *mise en scène* of blaxploitation films. The location is usually the decayed inner-city ghetto. Costumes tend towards the more outlandish extremes of 70s' fashion – bright colours, wide-brimmed hats, flared trousers and ostentatious jewellery (the title sequence of *Foxy Brown* is a useful example). Hairstyles are commonly the 'natural' or Afro.

Certain actors became famous for their appearances in these films, much as Clint Eastwood is still associated with Westerns: Antonio Fargas, Raymond St Jacques, D'Urville Martin, Fred Williamson, Yaphet Kotto, Jim Kelly and many others appeared in countless blaxploitation movies. And although women were often poorly served by blaxploitation in terms of their subsidiary roles and sexualised appearance, there had never before been a screen actress like Pam Grier, who was allowed to triumph by physically taking on the men and beating them at their own game.

The soundtracks are also distinctive, being a mixture of soul, jazz and funk, and featuring top black music artists of the day such as Isaac Hayes, Curtis Mayfield, Willie Hutch, J J Johnson and Herbie Hancock.

Other genres were adapted for use in blaxploitation films, particularly towards the end of the cycle. These include martial arts (*Three the Hard Way*, Gordon Parks Jr, US, 1975), horror (*Dr Black, Mr Hyde*, William Crain, US, 1976), comedy (*Dolemite*, D'Urville Martin, US, 1975), fantasy (*Space Is the Place*, John Coney, US, 1974), costume drama (*Mandingo*, Richard Fleischer, US, 1975), and even the Western (*Take a Hard Ride*, Antonio Margheriti, Italy/US, 1975). It is worth discussing whether certain genres lend themselves to the exploitation style more effectively than others. Teachers able to obtain copies of blaxploitation films could also use them to compare and contrast their versions of familiar genres with more conventional Hollywood examples.

Although *Shaft* and *Superfly* are the best-known examples of blaxploitation, the first and most notorious film in the series was *Sweet Sweetback's Baadasssss Song*.

● *Sweet Sweetback's Baadasssss Song*

Teachers are advised to check the content of this film for suitability before screening any of it to students, since it still has the power to shock: the opening shows a young black street urchin (played by Mario Van Peebles, the director's 13-year-old son) being sexually initiated by a prostitute. He becomes an employee of the brothel. Now an adult (played by Van Peebles senior), Sweetback one night sees the police beat up a young black activist known as

Moo Moo. Sweetback responds to this brutality by attacking them in return and freeing Moo Moo. The two go on the run. At one point Sweetback kills two police officers to avoid capture.

Moo Moo and Sweetback split up. The manhunt, orchestrated by a ruthless and publicity-hungry police commissioner, grows more intense. After a long pursuit by the forces of law and order through city and desert, during which he is shielded by a variety of local people, Sweetback finally escapes from a pack of ferocious tracker dogs, and makes it across the river to safety in Mexico. At the end a title zooms out of the screen:

> Watch out – WATCH OUT – A Baadasssss Nigger Is Coming Back to Collect Some Dues.

Melvin Van Peebles' film has been accused of sexism, of peddling black stereotypes, of trashy sensationalism and gimmicky special effects. Yet it has also been described as an authentic black American film, and even on occasions as an art film. In fact, although *Sweet Sweetback* undoubtedly influenced a generation of black filmmakers, when re-examined in a broader historical and international context, it looks less like a blaxploitation film, but something more serious, thoughtful and multilayered than such films as *Shaft* or *Foxy Brown*. Its themes, styles and formal elements reveal affinities with the forms and practices normally associated with art, avant-garde, auteur and, in particular, Third Cinema in other countries. Certainly it is an ideal candidate for numerous options in Film Studies Paper FS6: Experimental Film-Making or Shocking Cinema in section A; Regulation and Censorship or Independent Film and its Audience in section B; and almost any of the section C options.

Van Peebles trained as a film director in Paris during the mid-1960s at a time when Jean-Luc Godard was building on the experimental techniques first used in his *nouvelle vague* classic *A Bout de Souffle* (*Breathless)* (France, 1959). It is worth considering what idea might lie behind the quotation used as screen text at the start of *Sweet Sweetback's Baadasssss Song*:

> not a homage to brutality ... but a hymn from the mouth of reality.

And of course the word 'song' might imply a film structure which is more poetic than realist.

Van Peebles' stated intention was to create a revolutionary film which would at the same time prove accessible and entertaining for a black audience. And in the enigmatic character of Sweetback he presented an iconic hero/anti-hero figure who takes on the white establishment on behalf of the black community, and wins. (Teachers may wish to discuss the post-war idea of the anti-hero, and how it differed from the traditional hero.) By contrast, the protagonists of blaxploitation films like *Shaft* and *Superfly* do not seek to challenge 'the system': they are individualists working either within it for professional ends or around it for personal ends.

Sweet Sweetback's Baadasssss Song also provides an interesting example of independent filmmaking. It was financed with around $100,000 of Van Peebles' own money, mostly derived from directing *Watermelon Man* (US, 1970) for Columbia Pictures, along with an additional $50,000 from the actor Bill Cosby. A variety of cost-cutting measures were also employed. These included deferral of location equipment and laboratory costs, along with the use of Columbia's sound-dubbing facilities. The cast were non-professionals, and the crew non-union. It was in order to avoid union problems that the film was made covertly: the pretence was maintained that it was a routine pornographic production, on which such niceties as union membership did not apply.

It was shot on 16mm in 19 days of almost continuous activity during May and June 1970, using two cameras because for Van Peebles it allowed speed and flexibility when working with non-professional actors. The director had originally been set on using 35mm because he was determined

> that the film was going to look as good as anything one of the major studios could turn out. (Van Peebles, 1996)

Later he realised that 35mm was out of the question.

> 16mm is more grainy, less slick than 35mm, ie more newsreely, more documentary. The more I thought about it, the more I felt 16 would even add to the flavor of realism I wanted in the street. (ibid)

Editing began immediately after shooting, and was completed by November.

Van Peebles was determined to retain ownership and control of his film; rather than sell it outright he elected to lease it to Cinemation, a small distributor of exploitation movies. The involvement of Cinemation has provided ammunition for those who have questioned Van Peebles' motives. At least one critic considered that the film's independence was fatally compromised by Cinemation's involvement, going so far as to accuse the director of intensifying the sexual content to keep them happy. Van Peebles arranged a record deal for the soundtrack album with Stax Records. He then embarked on a high-profile dispute with the Motion Picture Association over its request for him to self-apply an X rating to the film, since he had refused to submit it for certification on the grounds that to do so would constitute 'prior censorship'.

Since there were no black-owned exhibition chains, and nearly every cinema refused to show the film, *Sweetback*'s opening was limited to one theatre in Detroit and another in Atlanta. In both cases it broke the house record. Following a promotional and advertising campaign by its producer, the film re-emerged with a second wave of openings in the autumn, beginning in the New York area. Eventually *Sweetback* was shown nationwide in over 200 cinemas. See **Worksheet 7** (p29).

Case study 4: Auteur director study – Spike Lee

● Context and historical background

Whatever the commercial and artistic ups and downs of his later career, Spike Lee has always striven to preserve his independence from Hollywood in order to continue making controversial films with a personal vision. As, variously, writer, producer and actor in his own films as well as director, Lee exerts more personal control over the finished product than most. Since he first enjoyed success with *She's Gotta Have It* (1986), every movie has been made by his own production company 40 Acres and a Mule Filmworks, and many of them are set in his home neighbourhood of Bedford-Stuyvesant in Brooklyn, New York.[18] He has often employed family members on film projects including his musician father Bill Lee, who scored four of his early films, brothers David and Cinqué, and sister Joie.

A loose repertory company of actors has provided a regular pool of talent for Spike Lee films, among them Ossie Davis, John Turturro, Samuel L Jackson, Michael Imperioli and Bill Nunn. Both producer Jon Kilik and composer Terrence Blanchard have worked with Lee on 12 productions. Other key collaborators have included cinematographer Ernest Dickerson (seven), costume designer Ruth Carter (nine), and production designer Wynn Thomas (11). Numerous other crew members were given their first opportunities in the film industry by Spike Lee.

All of this has helped to develop continuity of theme and style across Lee's body of work, compared with the careers of many other directors who move from one unrelated project to another, often working in a variety of genres with different collaborators. A Spike Lee film (or 'joint') is usually far from the straightforward entertainment product routinely produced in Hollywood. The hard-hitting, sometimes uncomfortable subject matter has often restricted his audience and hence the box-office receipts of his films. This in turn has limited the budgets of subsequent projects.

In order to identify a genuine auteur we must be able to detect common factors – motifs or trademarks – which appear throughout the director's work. According to the original proponents of auteur criticism, film as a primarily visual medium should be judged in terms of its *mise en scène*. We have already referred to Spike Lee's repeated use of Brooklyn locations and the

---

[18] In both *The Birth of a Nation* and *Gone with the Wind*, white abolitionists address freed black slaves in front of signs reading '40 Acres and a Mule'. In *Gone with the Wind*, the abolitionist declares: 'We're going to give every last one of you forty acres and a mule. And you're going to become voters! And you're going to vote like your friends do!' There was some historical truth in the making of this promise, but in reality few if any ex-slaves ever received land or mules, and the phrase has come to represent the failure of post-war Reconstruction in helping black people build new lives.

characters who typically inhabit its streets. In some films he has made use of unusual visual effects: for example, his 'gliding' shot of characters walking down the street in *Jungle Fever* (US, 1991). Colour saturation is a feature of both *Do the Right Thing* and *Clockers* (US, 1995). However, it is really in his themes that Lee's distinctive trademarks emerge.

The question of ethnicity is at the forefront of these themes. Lee's preoccupation with matters of race has dominated all but a few of his films, which in addition to *Malcolm X* (US, 1992) have dealt with black–white sexual relationships (*Jungle Fever*), drugs (*Clockers*), jazz (*Mo' Better Blues*, US, 1990), black family life (*Crooklyn*, 1994), race riots (*Do the Right Thing*), black representation (*Bamboozled*), a black political rally (*Get on the Bus*, US, 1996) and a documentary about the Civil Rights movement (*4 Little Girls*, US, 1997).

External or biographical factors can also throw light on an auteur. Spike Lee clearly believes he has a social responsibility not only as a film director but as a black man. He has become embroiled in a number of high-profile controversies, the most famous of which was his objection to the repeated use of the world 'nigger' in Quentin Tarantino's *Pulp Fiction* (US, 1994) and *Jackie Brown* (US, 1997).[19] This is satirised in *Get on the Bus*, where a Republican-voting black car dealer uses the word in every sentence before being thrown off the bus. Lee also described *The Patriot* (Roland Emmerich, US, 2000), set during the American war of independence, as 'a complete whitewashing of history' because it ignored slavery and the genocide inflicted on Native Americans. He is also a strong believer in the work ethic and has not been afraid to criticise black American men for what he sees as irresponsibility in such matters as drugs and sexual behaviour. The title sequence of *Get on the Bus*, in which images of chains and shackles are mixed with those of handcuffs, makes explicit the link he sees between black criminality and slavery. The final speech by George, the bus driver, is an impassioned plea for better behaviour by black men.

More recent Spike Lee films have focused less on race issues or even black characters: *Summer of Sam* (US, 1999) and *The 25th Hour* (US, 2002) both feature a largely white cast, although the stories are once again set in New York. Although somewhat offbeat, *Inside Man* (US, 2006) is more of an urban heist thriller than a film about a black policeman.

---

[19] Ashley Walters, star of *Bullet Boy*, used to utter the N word frequently but changed his mind after researching it for the Channel 4 programme *Sticks and Stones* (2005).
'I can sit here and say we're reclaiming the word but a lot of things don't make sense about it. For example, to this day you hear black people putting each other down with it … I began to understand that you can't say that a word means one thing coming from black people's lips but has another meaning when it comes from a white person's … I didn't know it was the word of the slave master, intended to dehumanise black people and make them feel unworthy of the respect and rights that human beings deserve …'

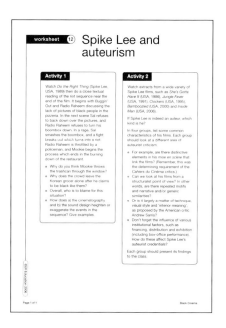

Lee's espousal of progressive causes has to be seen in the context of his work for such business clients as Nike, Diet Coke and Levi's, conducted nowadays through his advertising agency Spike/DDB. For Nike he has reprised his role as the character Mars Blackmon from *She's Gotta Have It* in a number of commercials with the basketball star Michael Jordan. His relationship with the company has remained strong despite Nike admitting to the exploitation of workers making its products in Third World sweatshops while paying Jordan $20 million to endorse the brand.

Amiri Baraka (1993) describes Spike Lee as

> the quintessential buppie … a Black, petit bourgeois professional.

According to him, Lee has no proper class-consciousness. Even Lee's official biographer comments:

> It seems that Spike's love of basketball and his respect for business have wrought a certain kind of havoc upon his beliefs. (Aftab, 2005)

He has also made a number of music videos for acts such as Public Enemy and Arrested Development, and operates his own store selling merchandise from the films. See **Worksheets 11** and **12**.

● *Do the Right Thing*

Many consider this film, Spike Lee's third full-length feature, to be his finest. A number of well-publicised episodes of racial violence inspired him to write the script, particularly the Howard Beach Incident, which took place in Bensonhurst, a white neighbourhood in the New York borough of Queens. Three young black men were attacked by a mob of white teenagers after leaving a pizza restaurant, and one of them – Michael Griffith – was killed.

The film takes place on a single city block of Bedford-Stuyvesant on the hottest day of the year. Sal, an Italian-American, runs a pizza restaurant with his sons Pino and Vito. The delivery boy is Mookie, a young black man played by Spike Lee. The walls inside the pizzeria are decorated with photographs of famous Italian-Americans like John Travolta, Rocky Marciano and Frank Sinatra. But his clientele is almost entirely black, and a dispute breaks out over why there are no 'brothers' on the wall. The argument boils over into a major riot, during which one of the protesters is killed and the restaurant is torched. In a scene reminiscent of Eisenstein's *Strike* (USSR, 1925), the firemen who arrive to quench the flames turn their hoses on the rioters.

The next day Mookie finds Sal sitting outside the burned-out wreckage of his pizzeria and demands his week's wages. The film ends with two quotations about violence – one from Martin Luther King condemning it as self-defeating, and another from Malcolm X calling it a legitimate response when carried out in self-defence. The final shot is a still black-and-white photograph of the two leaders together, smiling broadly.

It was originally intended that Paramount Pictures would finance and distribute the film, but they objected to the ending, and so the project was picked up by Universal. Spike Lee decided in the interests of realism to shoot the film on location in Bedford-Stuyvesant. The pizzeria and the Korean grocery opposite were specially constructed on facing vacant lots. Following his usual practice Lee hired black Americans for many of the crew, and asked a black Muslim group, the Fruit of Islam, to clear the block of drug dealers and users, and provide security for the shoot. Local people were also hired to help with such tasks as construction and to perform as extras in the crowd scenes.

Lee had heard that once the temperature reaches 35 degrees Celsius, the murder rate increases accordingly. The production design and cinematography were therefore intended to convey a feeling of intense heat. As cinematographer Ernest Dickerson explains on the 'making of' documentary on the DVD, the brightest possible colours were used for the costumes and the set – in this case, in an expressionist rather than a realist way, to stimulate the emotions of the audience.

The title sequence features Rosie Perez dancing energetically, even angrily, sometimes wearing boxing gloves, against a changing night-time backdrop of city buildings. The musical accompaniment is the tune heard throughout the film – 'Fight the Power', by the group Public Enemy. The lyrics reflect the angry, frustrated themes of the film, with such lines as 'most of my heroes don't appear on no stamps' (the pizzeria bears the name 'heroes').

Conflicts bubble up constantly in the film, not only between the blacks and the Italians but between Mookie and his girlfriend Tina, who has given birth to his baby; between the racist Pino and the easy-going Vito; between the old black men who sit around doing nothing all day and the Korean storeowners, patrolling police officers and younger black characters; between Radio Raheem and the Latino youths; between Buggin' Out and the white cyclist who runs over his brand new Nike Jordans.

In the uproar which surrounded the film's release, Spike Lee was accused of inflaming racial tension. He claims that

> we tried to go for the truth rather than worry about whether it's positive or negative.

Regarding any suggestions of promoting any particular point of view:

> I think it would be false for me to provide answers to stuff that I don't know the answers to. I'd be abusing the medium of film.

(See also the representation exercise on p33.)

Case study 5: Star study – Denzel Washington

● Context and historical background

Best known for a series of quiet, controlled, dignified performances since he began his screen acting career in 1981, Denzel Washington's most significant – and unprecedented – public achievement as a black actor has been to win two Oscars and three further nominations. Thanks to his handsome looks and 'decent' screen persona he has been compared with Sidney Poitier. However, it was in the role of Alonzo Harris, a corrupt narcotics officer in *Training Day* that he won his 2002 Oscar for Best Actor. His first, for Best Supporting Actor, was in *Glory* (Edward Zwick, US, 1989).

Denzel Washington has long since acquired the 'commodity value' to be considered a true star – defined as an actor who can carry a film in the absence of any other star; whose presence ensures that a new film will, at the very least, receive substantial media attention after which critics and audiences will then make up their own minds about its quality and entertainment value. Earning a reputed $20 million per film, Washington currently vies with Will Smith as the highest-paid black star.

When we consider the notion of stardom, one of the most difficult elements to pin down is image. In the studio era stars became known for certain genres – John Wayne in Westerns, Humphrey Bogart in noirs, Dorothy Lamour in comedies. In modern times actors have greater control over their own careers: free to negotiate with any producer, they have become an essential element of any 'package' designed to attract finance from investors. Wherever possible, stars try to avoid becoming typecast: acting careers can be sustained for longer if they can be considered for a wide range of roles. Concerned about typecasting in recent years, Denzel Washington reportedly announced in 2004 that from then on he intended only to play villains (though this may have been tongue in cheek, judging by his subsequent roles, eg *Inside Man*).

After a middle-class childhood in New York State he gained a degree in journalism, but after graduation went to San Francisco to study acting at the American Conservatory Theatre. He first came to wide public notice as Dr Philip Chandler in TV's *St Elsewhere*, in which he was a fixture from 1982 to 1988. In *Glory*, alongside Morgan Freeman, he played Trip, an escaped slave who joins a black regiment fighting for the North in the Civil War, and becomes one of its leaders, largely by speaking out against the racism he encounters. While critical reaction to the film was favourable, some reviewers noted that the story – one of black experience – is largely told from the point of view of the regiment's white commanding officer.

But it was in roles as two historic black leaders that his screen persona became established: in the British-made *Cry Freedom* (Richard Attenborough, UK, 1987) he played the apartheid-era icon Steve Biko, and in 1992 he was Spike Lee's Malcolm X.

Stars often seem to fulfil a need in the audience depending on the mood of the times. After the blaxploitation years came the era of the foul-mouthed black comedy stars Richard Pryor and Eddie Murphy. The emergence of someone who could play more positive black role models therefore may have seemed what was required in the early 1990s when Washington came to the fore.

As a jazz trumpet player in Spike Lee's *Mo' Better Blues*, Washington portrayed a successful, talented character whose main problems are self-absorption and lack of commitment in his private life. By the end of the film he has given up his music career to become a solid family man. In *Malcolm X*, he succeeds in making the controversial firebrand black politician seem likeable as well as serious.

There is a neat reversal of the traditional black role as the object of bigotry in *Philadelphia* (Jonathan Demme, US, 1993), in which he plays an ambulance-chasing lawyer. Washington adopts the position of the heterosexual audience member with all the 'normal' homophobic tendencies. As he comes to know the gay character played by Tom Hanks, he comes to realise that his bigotry and fear are being undermined.

Washington has been aware of the pitfalls of playing too many noble and uncontroversial roles by frequently appearing in films which, like *Malcolm X* and *Philadelphia*, carry social and political themes: in the remake of *The Manchurian Candidate* (Jonathan Demme, US, 2004), the Communist threat of the original 1962 film has been replaced by the equally sinister subversion of democracy by multinational corporations and the rightwing politicians who serve their interests.

Washington plays Major Ben Marco, in charge of a Gulf War army unit who are captured and brainwashed. Once again his character is fighting a lonely campaign against institutional corruption and conspiracy, during which his sanity is at stake, although this sweaty, haunted performance is less intense and intelligent than his portrayal of Rubin Carter in *The Hurricane* (1999).

As often as he has played characters who are at least partially defined by their race, eg in *Devil in a Blue Dress* (Carl Franklin, US, 1995) and *The Hurricane*, Washington has been allowed by Hollywood's more racially open spirit of recent years to play leading roles in which race is not on the agenda, such as *Crimson Tide* (Tony Scott, US, 1995) and *The Bone Collector* (Phillip Noyce, US, 1999) – despite the presence in the latter of a black female co-star, Queen Latifah.

Almost absent from his screen career to date have been scenes featuring sex and romance. Despite his obvious potential in this area, he is said to feel uncomfortable performing in such scenes. According to Donald Bogle, black women in the audience booed when he became involved on screen with white actresses Mimi Rogers (in *The Mighty Quinn*, Carl Schenkel, US, 1989) and Milla Jovovich (*He Got Game*, Spike Lee, US, 1998). And despite the suggestion in *The Manchurian Candidate* that he becomes romantically engaged with Rosie, the character played by black actress Kimberly Elise, it remains no more than a suggestion. *Inside Man* ends with a rather coy and self-conscious bedroom scene between Washington and his black fiancée.

His Oscar-winning performance in *Training Day* plays firmly against type. Here he is a crooked narcotics officer who has lost whatever moral compass he may once have had, and is now indistinguishable from the criminals he stalks:

> It takes a wolf to catch a wolf.

He swaggers through familiar 'hood' settings with white rookie policeman Ethan Hawke, whom he calls 'my nigger', 'boy' and 'dawg'. Although his body language is as assured as ever, his facial twitches and crooked grin are new to his screen persona.

A good starting point for students would be to write a profile of his screen persona by watching extracts from a variety of films. See **Worksheet 14**.

To access student worksheets and other online materials go to *Teaching Black Cinema* at **www.bfi.org.uk/tfms** and enter User name: **blackcine@bfi.org.uk** and Password: **te2007bl**.

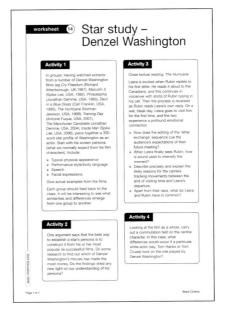

● *The Hurricane*

Potential champion boxer Rubin 'Hurricane' Carter is the subject of director Norman Jewison's film, with Denzel Washington in the title role. Focusing on a celebrated real-life miscarriage of justice, the film shows how Carter's prison career begins at the age of ten after he stabs a predatory paedophile (white) in the shoulder. He is imprisoned again for escaping from the juvenile correctional facility, then yet again, this time for three life terms, after a corrupt white policeman frames him for a bar-room shooting. Appeal after appeal is turned down.

One day a 15-year-old black boy, Lesra Martin, buys a second-hand copy of *The Sixteenth Round*, Carter's memoirs, and becomes obsessed with his case. He writes to Carter and meets him in prison. Lesra's adoptive white 'family' – three somewhat shadowy Canadians – lend a hand, and eventually all four devote their efforts full time to uncovering the evidence that will finally free Hurricane Carter.

The core of the film is the relationship between him and young Lesra, with whom he forms a close father–son bond. The point of view of the narrative begins with Carter, then alternates between them after the introduction of Lesra.

The film has a somewhat old-fashioned feel to it, ending as it does with a victorious courtroom scene. The fight sequences, all in black and white, are reminiscent of *Raging Bull* (Martin Scorsese, US, 1980), and early in the film these are intercut with archive footage of Civil Rights demonstrations. However, in this instance students should be asked to concentrate on Denzel Washington's acting performance in the role of Rubin Carter. This could be relevant, as could this case study as a whole, to the Performance Studies option on A Level Film Studies Paper FS6.

Before Carter meets Lesra, the film centres on Carter's struggle to retain his sanity in prison, particularly at the start of his life sentence when he is put in solitary confinement for three months for refusing to wear prison uniform. Several critics felt that Washington's raw performance was better than the script as, in the words of his voice-over,

> I made up my mind to turn my body into a weapon. I would be a warrior–scholar.

Later, as he tries not to weaken himself with false hopes of release, he tells Lesra and his helpers to stop their letters and visits.

According to interviews on the DVD, the making of the film had the full backing of the real-life Carter and Martin. This did not prevent criticism of it on the grounds of over-simplification and fictionalisation: there were not three but seven Canadians (nine, according to some sources) who lived in a commune; the real work was done not by them but by Carter's professional legal team, who worked *pro bono* for years yet hardly feature in the film; Carter married the female Canadian (played by Deborah Unger) after his release, but this is not mentioned in the film; yet again a screen black man achieves salvation thanks to white people; and so on.

It might also be profitable to compare *The Hurricane* with other prison movies in which noble black characters find themselves behind bars, eg *The Shawshank Redemption* (Frank Darabont, US, 1994) and *The Green Mile*.

Case study 6: Modern British black cinema

● Context and historical background

> Something needs to change, as we still haven't produced our Boyz N The Hood or unearthed our Spike Lee. (*bfm* magazine)

The following brief survey of the low-budget black filmmaking scene in the UK could be a starting point for the Independent Cinema option on A Level Film Studies Paper FS5.

We have referred earlier in this guide to the scarcity of black British representation and production in the cinema. In recent years it has been left to a handful of black writers and directors to create those few black-themed films that have reached the screen. Simple demographics may explain why this is: there are around 1.5 million people in the UK who describe themselves as either black or black–white mixed race, representing 2.8% of the population. Nearly half of these live in London. This compares with an estimated US black population of around 39 million, some 13% of the total. In short, the black American minority is far larger than the black British minority.

Even if we were to imagine that film audiences divide neatly along racial boundaries, the disparity between potential domestic film audiences in the UK and the US is clear. Producers and distributors in commercial cinema cannot ignore markets. Therefore films targeted solely at a UK black audience will always struggle to be viable without financial subsidy from such bodies as the UK Film Council, Scottish Screen and the Arts Council, and are likely to involve partnerships with the BBC or other broadcasters, or European sources such as Studio Canal.

In the early 1980s new funding for low-budget British films came from Channel 4 and the Greater London Council, whose aim was to provide opportunities for minority filmmakers. Filmmaking workshops emerged as a result, among them the Black Audio Film Collective, Ceddo Film and Video, and Sankofa Film and Video. (See **Worksheet 19**.) None of these survived into the new century.

FilmFour, an important source of funding, distribution and, ultimately, TV exposure throughout the 1980s and 1990s, closed its UK distribution and international sales division in 2002. However, it continues to fund up to ten small-scale independent film projects per year, with the emphasis on nurturing new talent.

To access student worksheets and other online materials go to *Teaching Black Cinema* at **www.bfi.org.uk/tfms** and enter User name: **blackcine@bfi.org.uk** and Password: **te2007bl**.

Although in some ways things have become more difficult for black filmmakers, in others they are a little easier. The availability of cheap digital camcorders, editing software and DVD mastering has put filmmaking within the reach of millions for the first time. Numerous short film festivals are held in different parts of the UK throughout the year, providing opportunities for new filmmakers to exhibit their work. In London, the annual *bfm* International Film Festival is in its eighth year showing a mixture of shorts, features, animation and documentary from black filmmakers in the UK and abroad. The British Film Institute also ran six months of screenings and other events across Britain in its Black World programme in 2005.

Despite greater TV exposure than before, students may also consider whether black British actors could be featured more often in domestically produced films. The UK's most successful film production company Working Title Films has been attacked for its failure to include black characters even in such films as *Notting Hill* (Roger Michell, UK/USA, 1999), set in a traditionally black part of London. Black commentators have also pointed out the missed opportunity of including the famous annual Carnival. Certainly, representation in mainstream cinema appears to lag behind television drama, in which black characters routinely appear in UK prime-time series like *Waking the Dead*, *Spooks* and *Hustle*, and soaps such as *EastEnders*. Occasional series like *Babyfather* have focused on the black community, and children's television shows like *Kerching!* feature a high proportion of black characters.

Despite the problems of funding and distribution, two films with significant black involvement – *A Way of Life* and *Bullet Boy* – reached the big screen in 2004 and 2005 respectively, and received critical acclaim. See **Worksheet 20**.

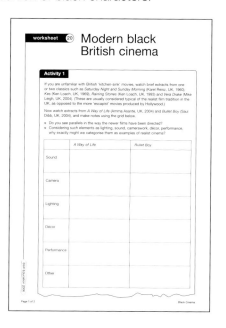

To access student worksheets and other online materials go to *Teaching Black Cinema* at **www.bfi.org.uk/tfms** and enter User name: **blackcine@bfi.org.uk** and Password: **te2007bl**.

● *A Way of Life*

Amma Asante won a BAFTA in 2005 for Special Achievement by a British director, producer or writer in their first feature film. This was for writing and directing *A Way of Life*. Asante, a black woman raised in South London, is a former child actor in TV's *Grange Hill* who went on to become a TV producer and writer. Her film confounds expectations in featuring no black characters. Instead it is set in a white working-class community in South Wales. Asante was anxious to avoid a simple black–white conflict, which for her would have eradicated the film's complexity.

In *A Way of Life*, Leigh-Anne, an unmarried mother, vents the frustrations of her bleak, poverty-stricken existence on Hassan, a Turkish man who lives opposite her, has been in the UK for 30 years, and is married to a white woman. The young men around Leigh-Anne – her brother Gavin, their friends Robbie and Stephen scrape a living from petty crime.

700 young people auditioned for the five teenage roles available. Stephanie James, as the central character Leigh-Anne, was felt to have the right combination of vulnerability and toughness.

Untypically, the film represents the situation not from Hassan's point of view but Leigh-Anne's. Students should consider whether or not the narrative positions her stereotypically as a racist. Although she is the cause and perpetrator of misery and racist violence, we are allowed to appreciate that she too is a victim, who needs someone to blame for her dire situation. Amma Asante says that Leigh-Anne's front window is like her TV screen, and the main thing she sees is Hassan.

If students have studied British cinema they should also be able to link the style of the film with other British movies made in the realist, kitchen-sink tradition. An important comparison, in theme as much as in style, is Ken Loach's classic TV drama *Cathy Come Home* (UK, 1966). Amma Asante has stated that among her influences are Tony Richardson's *A Taste of Honey* (UK, 1961), as well as the work of Mike Leigh, Spike Lee and early rap videos.

According to Asante, *A Way of Life* deals with hopelessness. Students should also consider the other themes that run through the film, for example, that of parenthood: the only positive thing in Leigh-Anne's life is the presence of her baby daughter. Her first hostile act towards Hassan is to scrape a key along his car after seeing him playing happily with Julie, his daughter. She and Gavin have no mother, and their friend Stephen has no father.

It is also worth discussing the confusion which exists over race in the minds of the characters: Stephen is half Indian, Julie is half Turkish. Both were born in Wales and look little different from their contemporaries but Stephen is accepted by the gang, while Julie is regarded as an outsider. As one audience member astutely comments on the imdb.com message board:

> The issue is roots rather than skin colour! [Stephen] had no involvement with his 'foreign' Dad so he feels Welsh through and through, whereas the girl was being brought up her Turkish Dad so in their eyes was only half Welsh. I think the race issue was meant to be ambiguous.

● *Bullet Boy*

Ashley Walters plays Ricky, a young black man just released from prison for stabbing another youth. As he and his friend Wisdom drive home to East London, they accidentally damage another car's wing mirror in a narrow street.

The altercation that follows leads to escalating tit-for-tat vengeance. Ricky tries to distance himself from the conflict but his misguided loyalty to Wisdom finally draws him in and he ends up using a gun to even the score. His younger brother Curtis sees where Ricky has hidden the gun and goes out with his friend Rio to play with it. Rio is accidentally shot, but avoids serious injury. Meanwhile, banned from the flat by his mother and shut out by his girlfriend, Shea, Ricky decides to leave the area, but gets no further than the station platform.

Born out of a BBC scheme to encourage documentary makers to turn their hands to drama, *Bullet Boy* was directed by Saul Dibb and co-written by him and the black writer Catherine Johnson. One of the producers, Marc Boothe, is also black. Reviewers have compared *Bullet Boy* to *Boyz N the Hood*, *La Haine* (Mathieu Kassovitz, France, 1995) and *City of God* (Fernando Meirelles/Kátia Lund, Brazil/France/US, 2002); according to its writers both its realist aesthetic and the idea of the two brothers were strongly influenced by Ken Loach's *Kes* (UK, 1969); the accident involving the younger boys was suggested by *George Washington*.

The project originated with a small production company Shine Limited as an outline story about two brothers. Having spent ten years writing teenage novels, Catherine Johnson was asked to help develop the story by creating a fictional family for the characters. Curtis was originally central to the narrative, but when Ashley Walters was cast as Ricky, the story began to centre on him.

Acting workshops took place over the summer before shooting started, and for the sake of authenticity dialogue was improvised by the actors, half of whom were non-professionals. It was then put into script form shortly before the scenes were shot. Students may notice that Curtis speaks a more conventional form of English than his older brother, who has adopted the street language and accent prevalent in London with working-class youths of all races.

Students should be encouraged to think about the plot, (familiar from many black American and World Cinema films about ghetto life as well as from British TV drama series such as *The Bill*): do they find the story stereotypical? If so, does this mean the characters and situations are equally stereotypical? Or are black characters so rarely seen in British cinema that the audience's sense of familiarity does not extend to all aspects of the film?

The concern for realism and authenticity certainly gives *Bullet Boy* a distinctively British feel. The director's background in documentary is suggested by the handheld camerawork, real East London locations and improvised dialogue. Students should also look closely at the cinematography and ask whether it looks like a TV drama or a movie, and if the latter, what are the differences?

The church service is an emotional scene, in which Leon the preacher testifies to his own previously bad life and how God helped him. The sound from this testimony and then the hymn tune 'Amazing Grace' continues through the cross-cut scenes in which Ricky finds Wisdom's body and prepares to leave, the sentiments clearly commenting on what is going on in his life. Do students detect any specifically Christian message here? They may wish to discuss the importance or otherwise of religion in the film or black people's lives in general.

There are unpredictable twists in the narrative: despite the inevitability that someone will end up dead, we cannot be sure who it will be. When Curtis leaves the church service, his reason for doing so is not clear, although his lack of participation seems to suggest disenchantment. He fetches the gun, but again we are not sure whether or not he intends to use it.

● The future of black British film

In considering how more films might be made about today's multicultural Britain in ways distinct from American cinema, Catherine Johnson believes the key will be for more black writers to come up with original ideas. (See **Worksheet 21**.) For example, black communities have existed in some parts of Britain for hundreds of years, yet black costume drama is one area where hardly any work has been done.

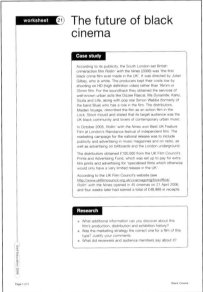

To access student worksheets and other online materials go to *Teaching Black Cinema* at **www.bfi.org.uk/tfms** and enter User name: **blackcine@bfi.org.uk** and Password: **te2007bl**.

Amma Asante feels that although scripts must be written with the audience in mind, writers must write

> from the gut – it's your voice and it's the only thing that distinguishes you from another writer.

Johnson identifies a problem that all black films have: their relative scarcity means that each one is expected to represent the entire culture. Not only that but the failure of one black film is often seen as a sign that such films are not worth making – despite the fact that 80% of white films disappear soon after release having failed to recoup their costs.

Some black audience members at screenings have expressed concern that black films featuring guns, drug dealing and irresponsible sexual behaviour give a bad impression to whites who do not know any black people. At the same time they harbour suspicions that a black romantic comedy or even an intelligent conversation between black characters would not make it past the white cultural gatekeepers.

Amma Asante points out that as a writer and director, her sense of identity and worldview are informed by the fact that she is black and a woman, and by the people she has shared her life with; nonetheless she finds the idea of black film in the UK difficult to sustain in Britain's multicultural society, in which black people do not only see black films.

Her advice to young people wishing to enter the industry is to be persistent and tenacious, not to regard single rejections as the end of the matter.

Swearing, sex, violence, drugs and racism are almost entirely absent from the films of Wayne G Saunders, a young black Londoner who has spent the last ten years making low-budget dramas and documentaries. He believes there are other sides to modern life that rarely appear on the screen, and it is these which interest him more.

His film *Caught Up* premiered at the *bfm* International Film Festival in 2005, his work having previously been screened at the National Film Theatre. His 60-minute documentary *The Gathering* won a Millennium Award from the BBC and ITN. This enabled him to make a film called *Greatness*: having met and filmed Muhammad Ali a year earlier, he found a way of using the footage to create a dramatic story about two boys' attempts to meet the legendary boxer.

As producer of his own films, he has successfully applied for funding from bodies like the Arts Council. Cast and crew are drawn from a wide circle of friends and acquaintances who are prepared to give up their time to help him out.

Like most young filmmakers, Wayne Saunders has the ultimate aim of making a properly funded and distributed feature. Meanwhile, he believes that the availability of cheap digital technology has ushered in a new era in filmmaking. At college and university he learned the techniques of production on both digital video and 16mm, but has found that digital is not only far cheaper than film but allows him greater flexibility in shooting, editing and mastering. He has developed an innovative editing style in which layers of images and sounds flow and overlap in a dreamlike manner. This approach is influenced in part by our modern experience of the world, in which media, such as personal stereo, combine with the outside environment to create a new kind of sensory headspace.

Saunders also runs video production workshops both within and outside London with people of all backgrounds – some of them as young as eight, to pass on the knowledge he has gained.

● Conclusion

The Washington/Berry Oscar breakthrough in 2002 was followed in the 2005 ceremony by Best Actor for Jamie Foxx in *Ray* (Taylor Hackford, US, 2004) and Best Supporting Actor for Morgan Freeman in *Million Dollar Baby* (Clint Eastwood, US, 2004). If this annual ceremony is an indication of the true industry status of black performers, it would seem that another racial barrier has now fallen for good.

Defining black cinema is, as we said at the outset, problematic. In illustration of this, it is worth considering two recent films – *Hotel Rwanda* (2004) and *Crash* (2005), which won the Best Picture Oscar for that year.

The independently produced *Hotel Rwanda* concerns the war between the Hutus and the Tutsis which left a million dead. As such, it is a film about Africa, set and shot in Africa. It stars a black American, Don Cheadle, and a black British woman, Sophie Okonedo. It was co-written and directed by a Northern Irishman, Terry George, Oscar-nominated writer of *In the Name of the Father* (Jim Sheridan, Ireland/UK, 1993). George was also one of the six producers credited. The other writer, Keir Pearson, is a white American, a former editor of documentaries.

George was unable to raise financing in Hollywood, so stars such as Nick Nolte and Joaquin Phoenix worked for greatly reduced fees to help ensure the film would be made. It was eventually funded and produced by a consortium of British, American, South African, Canadian and Italian companies, and a distribution deal signed with United Artists. Clearly the 'black' quotient of the film is high, but because of our diaspora definition, it does not fit easily into the categories suggested earlier in this guide. Perhaps the lesson for teachers is not to engage students in an arid debate over taxonomy, but to treat individual films on their merits.

Crash is an ensemble film (no single protagonist), co-written and directed by a white Canadian, Paul Haggis, who also wrote *Million Dollar Baby*. Don Cheadle once again features, and was also one of 14 producers of the film. As with *Hotel Rwanda*, Hollywood studios were not prepared to finance the production, and again, according to Haggis, the actors – including Sandra

Bullock and Matt Dillon – worked for minimal fees. The production went ahead independently through a consortium of small American production companies; the distributors, including Lion's Gate in the US and Pathé in the UK, were also independent.

The theme of *Crash* is racism but the ensemble is by no means neatly divided between whites and blacks, nor is the morality of the film a simple matter of whites being racist towards blacks, although this forms a part of it. The film is as much a comment on the impact of de facto racial and social segregation in Los Angeles (and by extension, the rest of the US). If anything, because of the mixture of races portrayed, *Crash* is less of a purely 'black' film than *Hotel Rwanda*, despite the presence of black stars Cheadle, Thandie Newton, Loretta Devine, Terrence Howard, Chris 'Ludacris' Bridges and Larenz Tate. It highlights an increasing tendency for black actors to thrust their way into the mainstream through less conventional routes when the subject matter is too uncomfortable for Hollywood studios. But, as with those films in which black stars play 'colour-blind' roles, it also suggests that the future may lie in films which are neither entirely 'black' nor 'white'.

Glossary

Alternative
Generally used to describe any film product, style, technique or production method that goes against mainstream Hollywood practice. Films that are experimental (eg **avant-garde**) or politically engaged may fall into this category.

American Civil War
Fought from 1861 to 1865 between the Northern (or Union, or Yankee) and Southern (or Confederate, or Rebel) states. The wealth of the South depended on their slave-labour plantations, of which cotton was the main crop. Fearful that the newly elected president, Abraham Lincoln, would abolish slavery, 11 Southern states seceded from the United States and formed their own independent Southern government, the Confederate States of America. Union forces moved to crush the rebellion.

Anamorphic
A widescreen technique that gives the director added scope to compose shots horizontally. A special lens squeezes the image during shooting and another unsqueezes it during projection. While creating a distinctively 'cinematic' look in theatres, this used to cause problems for broadcasters and video distributors before the advent of widescreen TV.

Auteur
The auteur interpretation of a director's role was originally put forward by young French film critics in the 1950s. Nearly always a director, an auteur is the supposed 'author' of the film, an artist with a personal vision to express. Under the Hollywood studio system, auteurs were those who, despite working within traditional genres, were able to create a recognisable personal style, visible in film after film. Only a minority of directors were considered true auteurs, eg Roberto Rossellini, Alfred Hitchcock, Howard Hawks, Orson Welles. Today's auteurs are more likely to be making **independent** films, eg John Sayles, Woody Allen, Spike Lee.

Avant-garde

Used to describe film form which 'pushes the boundaries' and challenges audience perceptions by failing to use the familiar, conventional techniques of image composition or storytelling. Today, any newly invented 'avant-garde' technique is rapidly absorbed into the **mainstream** through advertising, which uses it as a gimmick to grab audience attention.

Blackface

A tradition dating back to the 1840s in which white performers would blacken their faces with burnt cork in order to appear as singing and dancing 'nigger minstrels'. The minstrel show relied on a few specific black stereotypes, including the Coon, the Darky, the Wench, the Mammy, the Tom and the Pickaninny. Blackface continued in films, a famous example being Al Jolson in *The Jazz Singer* (Alan Crosland, US, 1927). In the UK, blackface was practised as recently as 1978 in BBC TV's popular *The Black and White Minstrel Show*.

Box-office gross

The amount of money received from paying customers at cinemas for any particular film. The gross for the first weekend of a film's release is a crucial indicator of its ultimate commercial success or failure.

Codes and conventions

Every genre has its own set of codes and conventions. Codes are visible or audible shorthand used in films to communicate instantly with the audience and save time: eg a close-up shot may signal strong emotion; sudden loud dramatic music can signal disaster. Conventions are whatever usually happens: eg car chases and gunfights are conventions of action movies.

Commutation test

A simple method used in Film Studies, for example, in order to assess the importance of an individual actor or star to a film role. The test consists of imagining someone else in the role and questioning how the substitution would affect our interpretation of the film, eg exchanging a particular black actor for a white actor, or vice versa.

Continuity editing

Continuity editing produces the illusion of continuous action in a film. It consists of a set of techniques designed to focus the audience's attention on the characters and the story by linking sound and vision elements together in a seamless manner; this allows the audience to forget that what they are actually watching is an elaborately constructed sequence of shots, each filmed separately over several weeks.

Cross-cutting

Invented in the early days of cinema, this is a narrative technique in which the action switches back and forth between two or more scenes to give the audience the impression that events are happening simultaneously in different places.

Defamiliarisation

One of the difficulties of teaching Film and Media Studies is that students are often familiar with the texts they are asked to study. This can result in a form of learning having taken place that then has to be unlearned in order for them to understand what they are looking at. The unlearning process is termed defamiliarisation and can be achieved through a variety of methods including detailed textual analysis.

Diaspora

The dispersion of a previously homogenous group of people from their original location. The slave trade created an African diaspora across the Americas. Today's diasporas are more often caused by civil wars or simply the search for a better life in the developed world.

Effects theory

The idea that 'vulnerable' members of the audience – ie the young and working class – are directly influenced by media texts, to the extent that it changes their behaviour for the worse. As such it tends to overlook the influence of other factors in the environment such as poverty, unemployment, poor housing, and the attitudes of family and peers. Traditionally the effects theory has been favoured by conservative newspapers, and forms a central plank of the 'moral panics' phenomenon.

Establishing shot

Conventionally each new scene in a film begins with a 'wide' or 'establishing' shot enabling the audience to see the dimensions and layout of the location, and the physical arrangement of characters within it.

Gatekeeper

A person who controls what gets into the media and what stays out. Such decision-makers include news editors, TV producers and film studio executives.

Hip-hop

For many years the world's most popular and profitable music genre, first given its name in the late 1970s, but only entering the mainstream in the early 1980s. Developed in New York's black South Bronx district by disc jockeys (DJs) who mixed together the instrumental parts ('breaks') of two records and talked (or 'rapped') over them.

Icon

Originally, in the Greek orthodox religion, a wooden tablet bearing the devotional image of a saint. Today used in connection with leaders and celebrities who are perceived to embody certain positive qualities, eg Martin Luther King as an icon of black leadership, dignity and peaceful, law-abiding protest.

Ideology

A set of beliefs, often characterised by the suffix 'ism', eg feminism, capitalism, socialism, environmentalism. For example, many advocates of Black Power embraced the ideology of separatism (or segregation) from white society, while others in the black community preferred integrationism. Racism is an ideology by which people's characters and abilities are assessed on the basis of their race.

Independent cinema

Any film production taking place outside the industrial complex usually termed 'Hollywood'. Such a definition would therefore include any film made anywhere in the world without the financial involvement of a major American studio.

Institution

An organisation exercising some degree of ownership and/or control over the financing, production, distribution, censorship, classification or exhibition of a film.

Kitchen-sink drama

A realist style of drama popularised in the UK by John Osborne's 1956 stage play *Look Back in Anger*, in which the previously dominant middle-class settings, characters and themes were replaced by those of the working class. British new wave films like *Saturday Night and Sunday Morning* (Karel Reisz, UK, 1960) and *This Sporting Life* (Lindsay Anderson, UK, 1963) also adopted the kitchen-sink style. Director Ken Loach is sometimes regarded as a modern exponent.

Mainstream

A term applied to the conventional, commercial films – usually, but not exclusively, made in Hollywood – which are the standard product designed for multiplex audiences. Also describes the **institutions** that produce them.

Messages and values

The **ideology** encoded within a film which is expressed through its representations, and which may or may not be consciously intended by its producers. These messages and values arc decoded by the spectator to create meaning for him or her. Spectators may sometimes resist the preferred (ie intentional) reading but usually they will accept it because they share the same values as the producers.

Middle Passage

The triangular route of the slave trade involved bringing goods from Europe to Africa to pay for slaves, which were then transported to the colonies, from which such commodities as cotton and sugar cane were then shipped back to Europe. The middle passage was therefore the one in which the slaves were taken to the New World.

Montage editing

A style of editing used in factual genres (eg documentary and news) and **propaganda** (eg advertising) in which the images do not flow smoothly and seamlessly as they do in drama, which normally uses **continuity editing**. However, the montage style is sometimes adopted for action sequences in drama.

Narcissism

A Freudian concept for the love and admiration we direct at ourselves. The term has been borrowed from psychoanalytic theory by feminist critics who apply it to male audience members' identification with the male protagonist of a film.

Nationhood

Refers to the idea of unity within a country. Often used to promote the social and political status quo, it is rendered problematic by the existence of minority races and cultures within that country that may not always share the values and traditions of the majority.

Negro, coloured, black, African-American

Terms used at different times in American, and to some extent British, history to describe people of African ancestry. 'Negro' and 'coloured' are no longer seen as acceptable because they embody past attitudes in which black people were regarded as inferior.

Nouvelle vague

French term for the 'new wave' of films made by young directors in the 1950s who rejected the existing style and themes of French cinema. New waves have also sprung up in other countries at different times, often reviving a moribund national film industry.

Objectification

The tendency to look at other people as things, as a means to an end, rather than as fellow human beings. Most commonly this refers to the objectification of women, when men regard them merely as a means of satisfying their lust. According to feminist critics such as Laura Mulvey, Hollywood has objectified women so routinely that 'the camera is male'.

Post-colonialism

Colonies are territories conquered militarily by states or acquired through treaty, usually with the object of building an empire (hence 'imperialist'). Post-colonialism therefore describes the condition of those territories or countries after the departure of the foreign occupiers, who often retain political, economic and linguistic influence over the former colony.

Postmodern

A notoriously fluid term used to describe a whole complex of practices and tendencies within modern developed culture, particularly media culture. These include pastiche, intertextuality, bricolage, consumerism, globalisation, commodification and the fragmentation of authority.

Production, distribution and exhibition

The three constituent parts of the film industry and the phases each film goes through: the financing, planning and making; the marketing; and the showing of the finished product to the audience.

Propaganda

Any communication designed to persuade its audience.

'Race' films

Films especially made for black audiences from the early 20th century to the 1930s, often by black producers. Production companies established included the Foster Photoplay Company, the Lincoln Motion Picture Company, the Frederick Douglass Film Company and, most famously, the Micheaux Film Company.

Scopophilia

Literally, 'pleasure in looking', and as such often used interchangeably with 'voyeurism'. However, scopophilia, according to Freudians, is a combination of voyeurism and narcissism.

Stereotyping

A practice used in all cultures to typify social groups by ascribing to them a set of easily recognisable features and tendencies, which are supposedly common to all members of the group.
Stereotyping is an essential part of social interaction as well as media production, and may be negative, positive or neutral in nature. Minorities and the less powerful are more likely to be the subject of negative stereotyping.

Structuralist

A mode of textual analysis which concentrates on form (eg a film's generic and narrative elements) rather than content as a means to reveal meaning.

Suspense, surprise and curiosity

Terms for techniques used by screenwriters and directors to retain audience interest in a film's narrative. Suspense is created by the delay of an expected event; surprise by a sudden, unexpected event; curiosity by speculation on the possible causes of events which have already happened.

Tag-line

Brief promotional phrase used on a film poster or in a trailer, eg 'The mob wanted Harlem back. They got Shaft ... up to here.'

Textual analysis

The breaking down of a film or sequence (text) into its component parts (eg *mise en scène*, cinematography, sound, editing) in order to reach a better understanding of its construction and possible meanings.

Voyeurism

The deriving of sexual pleasure from watching the object of desire, particularly when the person is unaware of being observed. Examples in cinema include many of Hitchcock's films, such as *Rear Window* and *Psycho*, and Michael Powell's *Peeping Tom*.

References and resources

Selected filmography

The following films are recommended for use in class. Spike Lee and Denzel Washington films receive prominence due to the case studies in the book. A complete filmography of all films mentioned in the book can be found on the website.

At the time of going to press, every film mentioned in this book was listed by imdb.com as being available on region 1 or 2 DVD or on VHS in Britain. Films are American unless otherwise indicated.

The Robeson films *Song of Freedom* and *Big Fella* are available as a double DVD. A few early 'race' films such as Frank Peregini's *The Scar of Shame* (1927) and Oscar Micheaux's *Within Our Gates* (1920) are available on region 1 DVD. Micheaux's *Body and Soul* (1925), starring Paul Robeson, and *The Girl from Chicago* (1932) and *Lying Lips* (1939) can be obtained from the US on VHS (NTSC format). The site http://acinemaapart.com/news1.html advertises a number of rarities on VHS and DVD.

Also included are a 1999 documentary about Paul Robeson, *Here I Stand*, directed by St Clair Bourne as part of the American Masters TV series; and Isaac Julien's 2002 documentary *Baadasssss Cinema: A Bold Look at 70s' Blaxploitation Films*.

Amistad (Steven Spielberg, 1997)
Baadasssss Cinema (Isaac Julien, US/UK, 2002)
Bamboozled (Spike Lee, 2000)
Big Fella (J Elder Wills, UK, 1937)
Big Momma's House (Raja Gosnell, 2000)
Birth of a Nation, The (D W Griffith, 1915)
Boyz N the Hood (John Singleton, 1991)
Bullet Boy (Saul Dibb, UK, 2004)

Burning an Illusion (Menelik Shabazz, UK, 1981)
Clockers (Spike Lee, 1995)
Coming to America (John Landis, 1998)
Crash (Paul Haggis, US/Germany, 2004)
Crooklyn (Spike Lee, 1994)
Daughters of the Dust (Julie Dash, 1991)
Defiant Ones, The (Stanley Kramer, 1958)
Do the Right Thing (Spike Lee, 1989)
4 Little Girls (Spike Lee, 1997)
Foxy Brown (Jack Hill, 1974)
Fresh (Boaz Yakin, 1994)
George Washington (David Gordon Green, 2000)
Get on the Bus (Spike Lee, 1996)
Glory (Edward Zwick, 1989)
Gone with the Wind (Victor Fleming, 1939)
Guess Who's Coming to Dinner (Stanley Kramer, 1967)
He Got Game (Spike Lee, 1998)
Here I Stand (St Clair Bourne, 1999)
Hitch (Andy Tennant, 2005)
Hollywood Shuffle (Robert Townsend, 1987)
Hotel Rwanda (Terry George, US/UK/Italy/South Africa, 2004)
Hurricane, The (Norman Jewison, 1999)
In the Heat of the Night (Norman Jewison, 1967)
Inside Man (Spike Lee, 2006)
Jungle Fever (Spike Lee, 1991)
Lethal Weapon (Richard Donner, 1987)
Malcolm X (Spike Lee, 1992)
Manchurian Candidate, The (Jonathan Demme, 2004)
Mandingo (Richard Fleischer, 1975)
Mo' Better Blues (Spike Lee, 1990)
Original Gangstas (Larry Cohen, 1996)
Pressure (Horace Ové, UK, 1976)
Rollin' with the Nines (Julian Gilbey, UK, 2006)
Shaft (Gordon Parks, 1971)
Shaft (John Singleton, 2000)
She Hate Me (Spike Lee, 2004)
She's Gotta Have It (Spike Lee, 1986)
Song of Freedom (J Elder Wills, UK, 1936)
Soul Plane (Jessy Terrero, 2004)
Sweet Sweetback's Baadasssss Song (Melvin Van Peebles, 1971)
To Sleep with Anger (Charles Burnett, 1990)
Training Day (Antoine Fuqua, 2001)
25th Hour, The (Spike Lee, 2002)

Undercover Brother (Malcolm D Lee, 2002)
Waiting to Exhale (Forest Whitaker, 1995)
Way of Life, A (Amma Asante, UK, 2004)
Zulu (Cy Endfield, UK, 1964)

Bibliography and useful websites

A much longer annotated bibiliography is available on the website.

● Textbooks, theory and background

Abrams, Nathan, Ian Bell and Jan Udris, *Studying Film* (Arnold, 2001).
Bordwell, David and Kristin Thompson, *Film Art: An Introduction* (7th edn, McGraw Hill, 2003).
Branston, Gill and Roy Stafford, *The Media Student's Book* (3rd edn, Arnold, 2003).
Buckland, Warren, *Teach Yourself Film Studies* (2nd edn, Teach Yourself, 2003).
Caughie, John (ed), *Theories of Authorship* (Routledge, 1981).
Cook, Pam and Mieke Bernink, *The Cinema Book* (2nd edn, BFI, 1999).
Corrigan, Timothy, *A Short Guide to Writing about Film* (4th edn, Addison Wesley, 2000).
Davis, Helen, *Understanding Stuart Hall: An Introduction* (Sage, 2004).
Dyer, Richard, 'Taking Popular Television Seriously', in David Lusted and Phillip Drummond (eds), *TV and Schooling* (BFI, 1985).
Dyer, Richard, *White* (Routledge, 1997).
Dyer, Richard, *Stars* (2nd edn, BFI, 1998).
Hall, Stuart, *Race, the Floating Signifier* (Media Education Foundation video, 1997).
Levine, Lawrence W, *Black Culture and Black Consciousness: Afro-American Folk Thought from Slavery to Freedom* (OUP, 1977).
Sarris, Andrew, *The American Cinema: Directors and Directions 1929–1968* (University of Chicago Press, 1986)
Turner, Graeme, *Film as Social Practice* (3rd edn, Routledge, 1999)

Much has been written about slavery and the slave trade. A useful educational website is http://www.spartacus.schoolnet.co.uk/slavery.htm.

● Films, filmmakers and stars

Aftab, Kaleem, *Spike Lee: That's My Story and I'm Sticking to It* (Faber, 2005).
Baraka, Amiri, 'Spike Lee at the Movies' in M Diawara, (ed) *Black American Cinema* (Routledge, 1993).
Bogle, Donald, *Dorothy Dandridge* (Boulevard Books/Amistad Press, 1997).
Bogle, Donald, *Toms, Coons, Mulattoes, Mammies & Bucks: An Interpretive*

History of Blacks in American Films (4th edn, Continuum, 2003).

Guerrero, Ed, *Do the Right Thing* (BFI Modern Classics, 2001).

Pierson, John, *Spike, Mike, Slackers and Dykes* (Faber, 1997).

Van Peebles, Melvin, *Sweet Sweetback's Baadasssss Song* (Payback Press, 1996).

http://www.blackfilm.com – general black film news and features.

http://www.filmsite.org/birt.html – *The Birth of a Nation*.

http://www.filmsite.org/gone.html – *Gone with the Wind*.

http://www.bayarearobeson.org/Filmography.htm – Paul Robeson filmography.

http://www.moviediva.com/MD_root/reviewpages/MDEmperorJones.htm – background detail about the Paul Robeson movie *The Emperor Jones*.

http://www.utexas.edu/utpress/excerpts/exdonbla.html – details of pioneer directors Gordon Parks and Melvin Van Peebles.

http://www.chicagoreader.com/movies/archives/0796/07126.html – background on Charles Burnett.

http://www.imagesjournal.com/issue05/features/black.htm – Charles Burnett, black independent cinema and neorealism.

http://www.bfi.org.uk/sightandsound/2002_08/feature02_FearOfBlackCinema.html – article on *Do the Right Thing*.

Several study guides are available from the Film Education website – click on first letter of the title. http://www.filmeducation.org/filmlibrary.html.

● Essays on aspects of black cinema

Diawara, Manthia, *Black American Cinema* (Routledge, 1993).

MacCabe, Colin and Cornel West (eds), *White Screen/Black Images: Hollywood from the Dark Side* (Routledge, 1994).

● Blaxploitation

James, Darius, *That's Blaxploitation! Roots of the Baadasssss 'Tude* (St Martin's Press, 1995).

Koven, Mikel J, *Blaxploitation Films* (Pocket Essentials, 2001).

Martinez, Gerald, Diana Martinez and Andres Chavez, *What It Is … What It Was: The Black Film Explosion of the 70s in Words and Pictures* (Hyperion/Miramax Books, 1998).

http://blaxploitation.com/ – large site.

● Gender

hooks, bell, *Ain't I a Woman: Black Women and Feminism* (Pluto Press, 1983).

hooks, bell, 'Sexism and Mysogyny: Who Takes the Rap?' (*Z* magazine, March 1994), available at http://race.eserver.org/misogyny.html.

Young, Lola, *Fear of the Dark: Race, Gender and Sexuality in the Cinema* (Routledge, 1996).

http://www.mahoganycafe.com/ – black women on screen.

http://www.aber.ac.uk/media/Documents/gaze/gaze09.html – useful summary of Laura Mulvey and subsequent discussion.

● Black British cinema

Bourne, Stephen, *Black in the British Frame: the Black Experience in British Film and Television* (Continuum, 2001).
Clarke, Nicola, Andrea King, Matt Ker, *Black British Film and Television: 16+ Guide* (BFI, 2000).

For teachers interested in further contextualising black film, every October is Black History Month in the UK: news, events and information about people can be found at http://www.black-history-month.co.uk/index.html.

http://www.screenonline.org.uk/ – essential resource for researching British film. Schools, colleges and public libraries also get access to video clips.
http://www.bfi.org.uk/education/teaching/blackworld/ – notes and resources on British black film, with detailed essays on *Pressure* and *Burning an Illusion*.
http://film.guardian.co.uk/features/featurepages/0,4120,1497374,00.html – article raising questions on British black cinema.
http://www.screenonline.org.uk/people/id/502424/ – article on Black Audio Collective.
http://www.screenonline.org.uk/film/id/445608/index.html – British black, Asian and Chinese film.
http://www.screenonline.org.uk/people/id/446731/index.html – Paul Robeson's British film career.
http://enjoyment.independent.co.uk/film/features/article307052.ece – survey of black British cinema.
http://www.bfmmedia.com/ – *bfm* (*Black Filmmaker Magazine*).
http://www.bfmmedia.com/bfmfestival/index.htm – *bfm* International Film Festival.
http://www.guardian.co.uk/g2/story/0,,1345771,00.html – interview with Amma Asante.
http://www.guardian.co.uk/arts/fridayreview/story/0,,1094352,00.html – location report on *A Way of Life*.
http://www.filmeducation.org/secondary/wayoflife.html – study guide to *A Way of Life*. While not aimed specifically at film or media students, it contains much detailed background and a host of questions about social issues related to the film.
http://www.bosscrowns.co.uk/the_ceo.htm – Wayne Saunders' website.

- **Black film histories**

http://www.indiana.edu/~bfca/clips.html – features very early (1890s) moving
   image clips of black subjects.

http://www.indiana.edu/~bfca/index.html – Black Film Centre archive.

http://acinemaapart.com/news1.html – detailed histories and rare black films
   from the 1920s to the 1950s, with some for sale on DVD.

http://www.greencine.com/static/primers/black-1.jsp – general black film
   history up to the 1990s.

http://www.brightlightsfilm.com/36/distribution2.html – article on US black
   films to date.

http://www.indiana.edu/~bfca/features/racemovies.html – race movies.

http://www.liu.edu/cwis/cwp/library/african/movies.htm – huge site with
   timelines etc.

http://www.phillyburbs.com/Blackcinema/stereo.shtml – black film history.

- **General film websites**

www.imdb.com – Internet Movie Database – comprehensive site.

www.bfi.org.uk – British Film Institute – lots of vital information about the UK
   film industry.

www.filmunlimited.co.uk – *The Guardian*'s film website – reviews and articles
   about current films.

www.suntimes.com/ebert/ebertser.html – thousands of film reviews by
   respected American critic Roger Ebert.

www.filmsite.org – useful, all purpose site.

Acknowledgements

First of all, I would like to thank my friend and colleague Bill Reiss for reading
the first draft of this book, raising a number of important issues, and offering
many helpful suggestions.

Several past and present West Thames College students helped enormously by
giving up their time and contributing information and ideas: Faridah Nsubuga,
Kimika Gardner (who kindly lent me some Jamaican and Nollywood films), Haley
Yearwood, Simba Ngei and Clem Neaves; and in particular, Jokae Ayoola.

Catherine Johnson, Amma Asante and Wayne G Saunders all generously
agreed to be interviewed for the UK section, and I am grateful for the benefit
of their experiences and insights.

Finally, Vivienne Clarke and Wendy Earle at bfi Publishing showed faith from
the start and helped me greatly throughout the process.